THE SAUNA AT TWELVE-FOOT

THE SAUNA AT TWELVE-FOOT

Collected Writings
Marlene Mattila Stoehr

The Sauna at Twelve-Foot
Collected Writings

Edited, designed, and composed by Valerie Stoehr
Set in Adobe Garamond and Monterchi typefaces
Back cover photo credit: Jerry Mevissen

Published by River Box Press
Afton, Minnesota

ISBN 979-8-9894991-2-0

Printed in the United States of America

Contents

Poems

Stories

Connecting with the Keweenaw

Endnotes

POEMS

Inheritance

My roots lie in alfalfa fields, blueberry woods and corn stubble.
In twigs from golden willows Dad fashioned into whistles, and
wooden slingshots powered with strips from worn inner tubes.
In tomato seedlings tended under the kitchen cupboard,
and smoky smudge pots, warding off September frost.

We played in the dusty granary-playhouse wearing
Mother's silk wedding gown sewn by Lizzie Franti,
and splendid dresses discarded by big-city aunts.
We wore darned socks, brown stockings over winter underwear,
back-to-school catalog specials, hand-me-downs from cousins.
We skated in man-sized skates with socks stuffing the toes,
and skied down frozen cow-manure piles
on wooden skis carved by Ed Peterson.

I remember horse-drawn machinery, the party-line telephone,
our gas-powered Maytag washer, the treadle sewing machine.
I recall the clamor of popcorn popping on the wood stove,
fudge cooling in the chipped oval platter,
Copenhagen snuff-can circles on bib-overall pockets,
Pearl Harbor Day, FDR's fireside chats,
butchering day and the day my grandpa died.
Only Aunt Minnie gave hugs. And our parents didn't cry,
even when they sent three sons to fight our country's war.

Coffee Can Treasure

In a family as large as ours, each child
remembers events that cannot be verified
by other siblings. For example,
I know that Mother showed us a coffee can
holding a 100-dollar bill on a cellar shelf.

When my pompous country schoolmate
tried to impress upon me that his family was rich —
and we were not — I envisioned that hidden wealth
and thought, "Oh, if you only knew!"

Recently, I mentioned this to my siblings.
They declared it highly unlikely that our parents
ever had such a large amount of cash during
the Great Depression. And even if so,
they envisioned no reason for it to be stored
in a coffee can on a cellar shelf.

Perhaps my siblings are right.
Perhaps there was never
a 100-dollar bill in a coffee can,
but for that one crucial instance
I was secure, and we were rich indeed.

Bath Night at the Petersons

Marks of the Old Country lay on the farm —
a small log barn with its straw-covered roof,
dried hay stacked on weathered wooden stakes,
small fields, tended with his sons.
Ed farmed as had his Finnish forefathers.

He was tall and gracefully curved
like the wooden skis he carved;
his wife, Effie, round and jolly.
Many Saturday nights Ed, my dad,
and the boys "took sauna" together.
Later, Effie and her daughter,
my mother and we girls bathed.

One wintry night, as hot rocks sizzled
and waves of welcoming heat enveloped us,
we kids, bare bodies billowing wisps of steam,
ran outside to roll in the newly fallen snow.
Our mothers sat upon two upturned washtubs.
And, just as Ed had imprinted
an old-world pattern upon their farm,
Effie stamped atop that galvanized washtub
a heart-shaped indentation in the glistening snow.

The Sauna at Twelve-Foot

On the banks of the Red Eye River,
near the deep spot known simply as Twelve-Foot,
stood my grandparents' sauna.
Gone. Not even the grass-lined path remains.
Gone. Pine benches and rag rugs and pine walls
where youth scrawled names and initials
with the cork from a bottle of Mrs. Stewart's Bluing.
Gone. Parades of people on Saturday night, carrying
fresh clothing in stiff, line-dried towel bundles,
partakers in the ritual that is the Finnish sauna.

A kerosene lamp cast light into the steam room.
There naked bathers on tiered benches
threw dippers of water at hot rocks cradled on the stove,
creating steam, cleansing steam, the essence of the sauna.
Switches, fashioned in early summer from leafy branches
and bound with a single supple branch,
released a summery fragrance as bathers beat their bodies,
making hot skin even hotter. A vent high on the back wall
opened to let in cool air and a chorus of river sounds.
Bathers lathered with pungent Lifebuoy soap,
rinsed with buckets of water from galvanized wash tubs.
They dried, dressed, stoked the stove with wood,
and refilled tubs with water from the Red Eye.

In the house, bathers complimented Grandma on the sauna,
as one might compliment a cook on her fine cooking.
"Such good steam tonight," they would say, while
sipping coffee through sugar lumps from large cups,
or from saucers balanced on two knuckles and a thumb.
A lamp cast a yellow circle before them as they spoke,
sometimes in Finnish and sometimes in English,
for some knew only one language, and some topics
were covered only in Finnish, in deference
to children playing in the darkened living room.
Last in the rotation, our family bathed. Then my father,
the oldest son, was entrusted to shave his father
and trim his mustache with exacting strokes of
the ivory-colored straight-edge razor. Sleepy children,
yet we watched, drawn by the aroma of the shaving soap
and the clink of the brush against the china cup.

Alone at last, my grandparents took their Saturday sauna.
As the fire died down they rested a bit on the pine benches,
then blew out the lamp and returned to the silent house,
together.

Heikki: 1860–1930

Midway to the farmstead
where our sheep are pastured,
we pause in the country schoolyard
for hurried moments on the monkey bars.
On this day of sweltering heat, thirsty sheep
wait at the moss-covered wooden water trough
where we will pump until they have their fill.
We make a game of our tiring task —
ninety-seven, ninety-eight, ninety-nine —
each in turn pumping one-hundred strokes,
counting aloud as the iron pump handle
becomes heavier and heavier.

No one lives here now —
darkened windows, silent house.
The sauna knows not the crack
of cold water on a bed of rocks
or the warmth of soul-satisfying steam.
We come only to tend the sheep
in this rugged pasture
where rocks protrude among hillocks
and lie scattered among the trees.
And we never stop to wonder about
the man whose home this used to be.
Just a name: Heikki.
Dad's immigrant uncle
who lies beneath the wind-blown pine
at the north edge of the country cemetery,
a weathered boulder as his headstone.

Blueberry Woods Symphony

We packed homemade bread,
a crock of butter, a stick of summer sausage,
a jar of pickled herring, a sack of sugar cubes,
cups from the cupboard, a knife from the drawer.
We filled blue Mason jars, some with water,
others with coffee whitened with cream.
By noon the water would be warmish,
the coffee lukewarm — a small price to pay
for a day in the blueberry woods.

In the forest undercover, powdery blue berries
grew with those yet pale green and purple.
Children mastered the art of coaxing only
ripe berries off a twig while claiming
frequent tastes of the tangy treasures.
Parents, aunts, uncles, cousins and siblings,
watched over by a crowd of curious crows,
orchestrated a blueberry woods symphony.
Light plinking followed by deep plunking,
then a muted melody as pails began to fill.

Of childhood summers of barefoot freedom
I recall nothing with greater nostalgia
than a day in the blueberry woods:
berry-blue skies, a warming sun,
the clatter of crows, the chatter of kin,
and tow-headed children with blueberry grins.

After the Funeral

Family and neighbors lingered
around the old oak table.
They drank cups of strong coffee,
ate bologna sandwiches,
nibbled at large squares of frosted cake,
talked about the weather,
and fell into prolonged silences.
They were delaying the time they must leave.
Everyone knew and no one wanted to say it.
Things had changed forever in that house.

Emma circled the table,
refilling coffee cups that were only half-empty,
then walked wearily to the window
and stood beside the wooden kitchen chair,
his chair.

Still dressed in funeral clothes,
without her usual apron
with a pocket harboring a handkerchief,
she reached for the hem of the ruffled white curtain,
gently wiped her eyes
and returned to serving her guests.

Seasons of My Childhood

Willow catkins, shy forerunners of spring,
whisper, "Shed winter underwear."
Buttercups bloom by swampy hummocks,
homemade kites trail rag-ribbon tails, and
chicks arrive in the mailman's Chevrolet.

Summer freshness follows rain as a
rainbow hangs drying in the eastern sky.
Barefoot, we splash in pothole puddles,
squishing soft mud between our toes;
at night chase glowing fireflies, by day
grow rich picking penny-a-can potato bugs
from Uncle Emil's field.

Autumn is the refrain of the saw rig,
the aroma of sawdust, wealth of a woodpile.
We buy Red Goose shoes with "room-to-grow,"
lined school tablets with movie stars on the cover,
and yellow pencils Dad will sharpen
with Mother's well-worn butcher knife.

Winter lingers. In the log barn, gentle Holsteins
long for freedom, anxious captives in their stalls.
The frozen manure pile remains our sledding hill;
snow-soaked mittens dry behind the heater stove.
The scent of potatoes sprouting in the root cellar
in time gives way to that of freshly turned soil,
alive with wriggly earthworms
in the garden of another spring.

Rural Free Delivery

I have scrutinized rural mailboxes.
A single mailbox on a husky wooden post.
Clustered mailboxes positioned on a plank.
Mailboxes affixed to braced wooden structures
or mounted to swiveling steel arms
to avoid demolition by snowplows.

I have revisited mailboxes of my memory.
A farmer's mailbox planted in a rusty milk can.
Dented and rusted half-ovals of steel
loosely nailed to wobbly pine posts.
Those riddled with bullet holes
made by inconsiderate youth with 22s.

It began on a country road when I saw
a woman stopped beside her mailbox.
As though we had exchanged places,
I perceived her keen anticipation,
a moment of expectancy
as she reached into that silver shell.

Mailboxes are icons of hope.
I have been one to approach a mailbox as to an altar,
genuflecting to the Postal Service required height
of 41 to 45 inches, bowing low one final time
to assure all contents have been retrieved.
Hope was tangible on that country road when,
the contents within unknown, I watched a woman
open her mailbox and reach for her mail.

They Also Serve

After John Milton's On His Blindness

Her scarecrow,
her loyal companion,
waits in Mangna's garden each day.
Not a dashing fellow,
expression unchanging.
A ragged shirt
hangs loosely on his jack pine frame,
flapping freely in any breeze,
fading in the summer sun.
Shoes? He has none.
Hat? Once yellow straw,
now brittle-brown and tattered.
On the job. Stalwart. Stationary.
Never hoeing weeds or digging potatoes.
Neither adding to the rock pile
nor harvesting bounty.
But loyal he is. Patient. Silent.
Serving as he was meant to serve,
waiting in her garden each day.

Fall's Fleeting Splendor

Tallest of all, the pious spruce
remain aloof, unchanging, oblivious
to the firestorm of color below.
Feathery, yet green, tamarack
and stair-stepped pyramids of pine
provide a sedate October backdrop
to masses of maple and oak,
their leaves afire with an internal blaze,
their crimson hues crackling,
their branches intertwining
with yellow leaves of birch.
The landscape mimics
an array of luxuriant carpets.

And Nature, having created
this annual show, will, so soon,
lay these patterns on the forest floor.

Onion Tears

Evening. Nearly mealtime in our farm home.
Mother was carving remnants
of Sunday's roast for hash.
One long ring on our wall telephone,
a call to Central on the party line.
I listened in. Everybody did.
It was this news I heard and had to tell:
"That was Mrs. Peterson. Ed just died."

Our neighbor, Ed Peterson, just died.
Settler farmers.
Our small farms were very near.
These parents shared the heartbreak
and the struggles of hard Depression years.
Pioneer Finnish families.
They neighbored. Shared grownup secrets
children's ears were not to hear.

But Ed just died, and I,
not yet conscious of the unrelenting rules of death,
came to understand the strength of friendship that day.
I learned that some emotions
run too deep to be expressed in words.

"Ed just died."
My father heard me.
He sat a moment,
then without a word,
left his paper on the chair,
moved to the table, and
began to chop the onions for the hash.

Point of View

I knew nothing about the skeletons at the end of that field.
Unwanted autumn weeds, they towered six feet tall,
gnarled, sturdy stalks displaying giant seed spheres.
I knew nothing of this plant's nature when growing,
giving rashes to humans and
poisoning cattle that chanced to eat them.
I only knew I wanted an arrangement
in a vase in our living room.

My Uncle Axel tended that field, a field his father had farmed,
a field like others where weed seeds sprout
where they are not wanted.
Perhaps perplexed, but too polite to say so,
my uncle gave permission to cut the stalks.
As I gushed, "Aren't they beautiful!
Aren't they beautiful?"
he simply, so kindly, responded,
"Well, I don't see them in just that way."

Farm Auction – 1979

AUCTION . . .
Located 3 miles west on Highway 87
to county line, then south 1 mile . . .
the following personal property . . .

A yellow auction bill — the final connection of kin to family homestead. Like a child arranging furniture in a dollhouse, I mentally place listed items in remembered places, reconstructing what the auction will take away.

My grandfather Jacob built this house, this barn, this sauna. On this farm he and my grandmother Elmina raised 12 children.

Soon the singsong chant of the auctioneer will rise over the crowd — family members steeped in nostalgia, neighbors sifting through remnants of the pioneering life their parents knew, strangers seeking bargains, antique lovers seeking treasures.

For the first time since 1903 someone other than family will own the farm.

Trunk

We are a family sprung from Finnish immigrants, the life of each grandparent a dramatic story, no chapter more desperate than that of Jacob and his family's departure from Pudasjarvi in 1867. At the peak of a devastating famine, eating bread made from tree bark for sustenance, they skied 400 miles to Norway in search of a better life.

The route along the frozen rivers was lined with bodies of those who perished along the way.

My grandfather Jacob, the middle of five children, was seven years old.

Dump rake
2-bottom 12-inch Allis Chalmers plow

The parents died in Norway; we know not where or when; too often immigrant families did not share those stories. Neither do we know how Jacob fared from a child of seven until he became a farmhand in Vadsø, Norway.

Sauna stove

My grandmother Elmina's parents had each made the same perilous journey. They met and married in Vadsø, a Norwegian town of predominantly Finnish immigrants who kept their Finnish ways, bathing in the community sauna, baking in the community oven. These Finns were referred to as Kvens, a term of derision. Norwegians knew this far-northern area would be difficult to defend should the Finns attempt to take it over. That was not their intent, however; they were only grateful for food and employment as farmers and fishermen.

Elmina's father worked on a Norwegian fishing boat, a dangerous occupation of which an adage bluntly states, "Few fishermen die in bed."

Globe with stand

In the 1880s many men chose to emigrate to America for economic, political, or personal reasons. In 1881, at age 21, Jacob joined them. He departed from Vardø on the storm-tossed coast of the Arctic Ocean, an area of multiple shipwrecks. Shortly before leaving Jacob was warned in a dream that his ship would sink. He begged in vain that a neighbor woman, also booked on that ship, not go. The ship sank; the woman was lost.

Not destined to die in a watery grave, Grandfather Jacob settled in the Upper Peninsula of Michigan where work was available in copper mines. Finns, usually inexperienced as miners, received the most arduous and lowest-paying jobs. Yet, possessing that character trait they called *sisu*, they persevered, determined to support themselves and their families.

In 1890, Grandmother Elmina, age 20, traveled alone to Osceola, Michigan, to marry Jacob, 10 years older, whom she had last seen when she was a child not yet 11 years old.

Copper boiler
Square-tub Maytag washer
Laundry tub rack

Elmina's parents and siblings also emigrated, and for a time the families lived together in a mining company house. Life changed tragically in 1895 when her father Isaac Haara died with 29 other men and boys in the Osceola mine fire, the worst mining disaster in Michigan's Copper Country.

Widows received no compensation for their loss. Elmina's mother was left with five children to raise. Shortly both families moved to Minnesota.

Jacob, born on a farm in Finland, employed on a farm in Norway, established this farm in Minnesota. Although faced with hardships prevalent at the time, he was a good farmer. He owned both a steam engine and a threshing machine and was among the first in the area to raise purebred cattle.

Double bit axe
Garden seeder
6-gallon crock
Rocking chair

Elmina, age 50, died May 3, 1921. Jacob, age 62, followed on April 8, 1923. He had lived in America for 41 years.

Sale starts at 11 a.m.
Lunch wagon on grounds.

Farm Home Supper

Seventy years married, most evenings
Anna fried potatoes in homemade lard
for herself and Ernie.
This night she fries for three —
her son, herself, and me.

She chops at sizzling slices
with her trusty aluminum spatula
(a premium from the feed store)
and steadies the wobbly handle
of the Priscilla Ware frying pan.

From my vantage point I muse upon
the circle of life, and note that the
curve of Anna's aged spine is echoed
in the matching curve of her bent
and long-serving frying pan.

Downsized

Beyond the wide window wall
the Great Blue Heron waded purposefully,
in perfect sync with
classical music on public radio.
Head sidewise, he peered intently,
then flung his beak toward hapless fish
swimming within easy reach.

On sunny days I might see him
stride toward the end of our dock,
then turn and spread his wings
to expose his inner feathers
to the warming sun.

Or, he might stroll in the dock's shadows,
lift and place his lengthy legs stealthily,
leaving no ripples upon the water.
He would often catch sunfish for supper
before flying away in his contorted posture,
head tucked between shoulders, legs stretched behind,
powerful wings flapping deliberately,
while calling out a rusty-pump song of farewell.

Today, from a smaller window,
I watch an iridescent, ruby-throated treasure
gathering sweet nectar. He hovers midair,
then, to my amazement, flits to sit
in the branches of the crabapple tree.
He looks back, black seed-bead eyes unafraid,
as if extending a welcome to the neighborhood.

Blood Lab Waiting Room,
Mayo Clinic, Rochester

Most patients assemble by twos in this cavernous room;
others sit alone, spaced apart like teeth of a jack-o-lantern.
Like them, I stare ahead. I wait. I watch. I worry.
I see the man a few rows ahead gently pat a shoulder
and smile at the woman in the wheelchair next to him.
On oxygen, she manages only a faint acknowledgment.
A man slouches feebly in a rolling chair, his crocheted cap,
a whimsical camouflage pattern, dangles from the handles,
swaying slowly back and forth from his any movement.
A pair of red suspenders drapes loosely over his shoulders.
Marked in one-inch increments to mimic measuring tapes,
they cause me to wonder if any medical test, any medical tool,
will be able to measure the length of his remaining days.
His companion nibbles on a crumbly muffin and sips from
a copper-trimmed thermos. A tortoise-shell clip seeks to hold
her thinning gray hair in a bun atop her head.
At irregular intervals an attendant emerges from the back,
reaches for the amplifying phone on the wall, and requests
a named patient to go to Door 1, or to Door 2, or to Door 3.
To some, this test will mean an end to hope, to others, a miracle.
For at this facility miracles can happen.
Here miracles do happen.

And each day, the scene repeats —
this gathering of the despairing,
this assemblage of the hopeful.

The Memory Tin

The button tin, who knows how long ago,
held a five-pound Hostess fruit cake.
Today, in the assorted glitter and practicality within,
I find reminders of a woman, insignificant by worldly standards,
who lived in three centuries, buffered by a courageous spirit
that carried her through 105 years.

We visited often in the 34 years we were neighbors,
frequently found her surrounded by sewing supplies,
the button tin beside her.
She might be recycling jet-black buttons on a suit,
metal crowned-eagle buttons on a coat,
or sewing pearl-button eyes on catnip mice
for her daughter's cat menagerie.

She was hesitant to reveal details of her life
yet we came to recognize the humiliation
at becoming a teen bride on her sixteenth birthday,
and a mother the day after.
We sensed the difficulty of life with a dominating husband,
her sorrow at being all but abandoned by this only child who,
secretly pregnant with Florence's twin granddaughters,
fled with her lover after a vicious confrontation with her father.

We perceived, bit by bit, the bitterness and heartbreak
she and her daughter caused each other.
Both now are dead, cut loose from a dysfunctional relationship
like buttons and buckles snipped from discarded clothing.
Both come alive again when I hold Florence's button tin.

Night Vigil

Stillness marked the passing hours
of the year's longest night.
Nurses glided in, gently glided out
with unspoken words of shared sadness.
Silence. Only silence. Pervasive silence,
under the ever-lengthening shadow of death.

Hour by hour the bleak night passed,
and at dawn of the winter solstice, a soul,
ever at one with the rhythms of God's creation,
also relinquished darkness to journey to the Light.

The gash inflicted upon the snow-blanketed earth
that it may receive the tired body will heal in time,
as numbed hearts also will heal,
as seasons renew from solstice to solstice.

The Visit

Now and then attendants add to, or subtract from,
the semi-circle of wheelchairs ringing the television —
nursing home mathematics.
Off to one side a couple sits at a table.
He holds an empty coffee mug;
her hands are idle, folded. Both are silent.
One is surely a resident — but which?

We whisper Ruth's name
and are rewarded with a
luminous smile of recognition.
She suggests we go to the quiet corner —
there by the man and woman will be fine.
We chat.
Where had we been? Where had we stayed?
Who had we seen? What had we done?

An adept manager of illness and heartbreak,
Ruth is suffering her final affliction.
She has no tales of activity to counter our full lives.
My heart weeps as she states in an accepting tenor,
"Life ceases to exist here."

Spurned Heirloom

Among cast-off items donated to
the Second Chance Thrift Shop,
I spied a shallow crystal dish
with a wrinkled note taped inside:
"Your great-grandma Bertha
brought this when she came over
from Germany in 1853."

I grieved for this woman, Bertha,
and for her unnamed descendant
who no longer cared.
What heart can be so small, I agonized,
that it cannot house this object, so valued
more than a century and a half ago?

Then I recalled the words of the poet
who wrote that you shall continue to live
so long as your stories continue to be told.
So I tell you of an ink-stained note,
taped to the crystal dish treasured long ago
by a woman named Bertha.

STORIES

Raised in a Chicken Coop

AARP's fiftieth anniversary ad read: "Founded on the simple premise that no one should have to live in a chicken coop."

I was born in a chicken coop and lived in that chicken coop until high school age. It didn't seem all that bad then.

Neither does it now.

My parents married on New Year's Eve 1920 and rented a small house near my mother's parents' farm. Two babies were born there. The little family shared its next home with my dad's brother, and soon bought adjoining acreage. The first building on the farm of their own was a 16-by-36-foot concrete-block chicken coop.

A third baby arrived, and so did the Great Depression. In time, the children numbered eight, and of necessity, the chicken coop, which never housed a chicken, housed a growing family. Buildings important to the farm operation were built. A log barn for milk cows. A hog house. A granary for field crops. An actual house had lower priority, always on hold, always in the future.

In its own way the chicken coop was rather charming, framed by a stand of poplar trees, a cluster of lilacs, and transplanted rows of wild plum and pin cherry trees. A magical moonflower bloomed at night, sweet pea vines climbed on a birch trellis, and zinnias and moss roses formed a mass of variegated color in my mother's flowerbed.

Free-range chickens, having lost the race for space, cackled from the grass to foolishly reveal their hidden nests. Up to 15 farm cats ruled the outer space, a wren sang from the birdhouse on the granary, and a friendly dog announced when a car drove up the long driveway. Likely as not our mother would say, "Girls, make a one-egg cake," or "Girls, make a two-egg cake," depending how much company food we had on hand.

The coop's 36-foot length was divided into three spaces: a kitchen, whose doorway led into the "front room," whose wider doorway led into the bedroom. In winter, fire in the wood-burning cook stove and another in the front-room heater warmed the house, yet the cold crept in. On the windowless north wall, furry frost outlined cracks in the concrete blocks; elsewhere frost painted delicate fern-gardens on windowpanes.

Space was at a premium. By the time my memories begin, a small screen-porch had been added to house the DeLaval cream separator and the noisy gasoline-powered Maytag wringer washing machine in warm months. In winter both were moved into the kitchen, the cream separator on one side of the door that we locked at night with a butcher knife stuck in the casing, the washing machine on the other. Mother's black treadle sewing machine with gold letters spelling out *Singer* spanned a window and stopped short of the first dividing wall.

The wall telephone hung there, its long mouthpiece our coat rack. When the phone rang two long rings for 1F7, our number on the party line, we lifted the coats and jackets from the mouthpiece and perched on the sewing machine to answer. If we wished only to rubberneck — listen to other people's calls to get neighborhood news — the coats remained in place as a sound barrier.

The cook stove, heart of any farm kitchen and resplendent in black with chrome trim, was centered on one kitchen wall. A reservoir at one end warmed water; we washed dishes in dishpans over that reservoir. On the stovetop we heated heavy flatirons, toasted bread, and popped corn in a long-handled popper. In the oven we heated bags of salt to warm icy sheets on wintry nights.

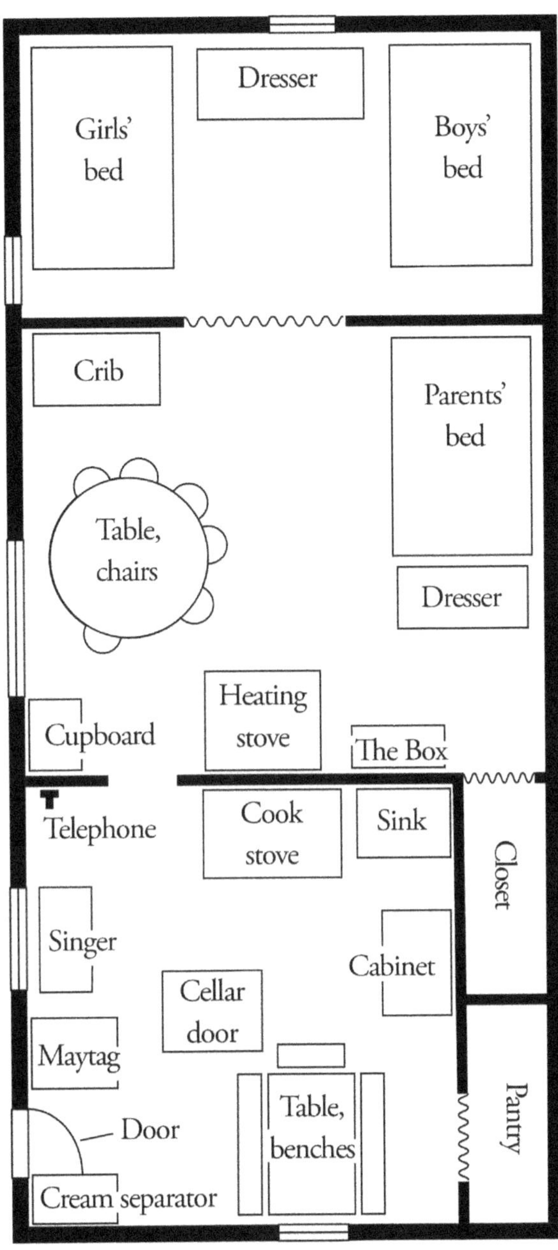

Our 16-by-36-foot chicken-coop home

Before we began to drive regularly to my grandparents for Saturday night sauna, we bathed in a galvanized washtub in front of the stove. Taking turns, youngest to oldest, we added hot water hot water from the teakettle to keep the water warm.

Our woodbox sat behind the stove, a hungry mouth waiting to be fed. While the older children helped with milking our small herd of Holsteins, we younger hurried to finish carrying in wood in time to listen to Jack Armstrong, All-American Boy, and hear the Lone Ranger ride again.

An iron pump stood over a sink in the third corner of the kitchen. Water drained into a galvanized pail and although we carried water out, we did not have to carry it from an outside well, as was common in the community.

Objects of both beauty and practicality filled the tall cabinet on the north windowless wall: a built-in flour bin with sifter, mismatched dishes and flatware, the much despised cod-liver oil in its oily brown bottle, a small pewter pitcher filled with wondrous bric-a-brac we kids loved to sort through, and a magnificent cut glass bowl received as a wedding gift that had held the water for all the children's home baptisms. In early spring, Mother started tomato seedlings in crates beneath the cupboard and baby chicks spent their first hours there after being delivered by the mailman. Weak baby pigs or frail bottle lambs were also nursed to health in the warmth of the kitchen.

Beside the cabinet, a curtain screened a pantry where we stored supplies of all sorts: bags of dry cereals, sacks of flour, kerosene in a metal spouted can, "farmer matches," and Red Wing crocks in which we made sauerkraut and dill pickles. Mason jars filled with canned vegetables from our garden, sauce from wild strawberries and blueberries, and juice from chokecherries, pin cherries, and plums waited here before being moved to the dirt cellar below a trapdoor in the middle of the linoleum-covered floor.

We had no electricity; a kerosene lamp lit the room with a yellowish glow. A rectangular table was pushed against the east wall; beside the table, backless benches. For many of my growing up years my oldest sister worked in the big city, so the family at home numbered only nine. Three children sat on either side of the table, my parents on one short end, and my younger sister on the windowsill at the other.

A square heater stove, a round oak pedestal table with wonderfully sprawling legs, and my parent's bed took up most of the space in the front room. Between the stove and a closet was The Box, a wooden bench with a hinged top, that stored items not used every day. Cast-off fur coats from my mother's younger city sisters and old overcoats that Mother sewed into children's snow pants and mittens took much of the tiny closet space.

The table in front of a double lace-curtained window was crowded with a kerosene lamp, a Philco tabletop radio, back issues of *The Sebeka Review* and *The Farmer* magazines, houseplant slips taking root in metal cans, school books, Montgomery Ward "wish books," and half-finished embroidery projects. Often a pair of knit woolen socks waited there for Dad to "turn the heel," a skill Mother never needed to master because Dad's Finnish-immigrant mother taught him to knit while he was bedridden as a child with the dreaded illness of poliomyelitis. Beneath the table were my little brother's lengths of wooden four-by-fours, his "horses," with names that echoed those of our father's and uncle's teams.

Chairs ringed the table, and it was there, after a hurried clearing of clutter, that company was served cake and coffee, so important to Finnish hospitality.

The youngest child's white iron crib sometimes filled the corner or sometimes traded places with the dresser and mirror at the foot of my parents' bed across the room. Cardboard boxes beneath their bed provided additional storage, one always full of socks with holes in the heel. My sisters and I learned to darn with the contents of that box.

A clothes rod spanning the double doorway to the bedroom held the family's entire wardrobe, pushed aside at one edge for space to walk through. My three older brothers shared the bed to the right, the bed I shared with my two sisters stood on the left, between them a dresser. There was just enough room at the end of each bed for a stack of old magazines and catalogs, precious material we used for cutting into paper dolls.

A two-hole outdoor toilet, furnished with prized peach wrappers and the remains of last year's Montgomery Wards mail order catalog, stood at the end of a path behind the house.

Those were demanding times for parents, with grasshopper infestations, fear of foreclosures, and acute shortages of hay and grain. But for children, protected from these grim realities, life was good. Fall and spring were times of eagerness for school to start and eagerness for school to end. Summer brought glorious barefoot freedom, splashing in puddles, swinging on the hay rope, catching fireflies, and playing house with cardboard boxes and old clothes stored in the granary.

Undaunted by circumstances, my mother held unto her deferred dream of a real house, some day. My parents pored over house plans from the lumberyard. But only after five of their eight children had graduated from high school did the dream become a reality.

Until a few years ago the chicken coop's concrete-block walls still stood. Of the eight children, today only my sister and I remain. We tell about our childhood to the younger generations, and, strange as it may seem, our stories never mention feeling crowded.

Christmas at Our Henhouse Home

This piece, written in June 2008, was the basis for "Raised in a Chicken Coop," page 37, which was published in 2016. Though the pieces are similar, this earlier version contains details about Christmas that are absent from the 2016 version.
—Editor

I did a double take last week at AARP's fiftieth anniversary ad: "Founded on the simple premise that no one should have to live in a chicken coop." I was born in a chicken coop and lived in that chicken coop until high school age. It didn't seem all that bad.

And neither does it now. Memories of those years run through my mind, none more vivid than those of being a child at Christmas. On the day of Christmas Eve we went with our dad to choose our tree from the stand of spruce beyond the pasture. We were children, little and close to the ground, and we chose our tree by looking high up in the treetops. When we spotted a seemingly perfect silhouette against the sky, Dad felled the tree and sawed off the very tip. The rest was left in the woods to dry for future firewood. Sometimes a treetop did not look as unblemished lying there on the snowy ground as it had when so many feet up in the air. We might have to cut down two or three.

My parents were married on New Year's Eve 1920 and moved into a small rented place near my grandparents' farm. Two babies were born there. They shared their next home with my dad's brother, and soon they arranged to buy adjoining acreage. The first building on that farm of their own was a concrete-block chicken coop, about 16-by-36 feet. As more babies arrived, so did the Great Depression, and the chicken coop became our home. Other buildings were built: A barn for milk cows. A hog house. A granary for field crops. These structures were important to the farm operation. A real house for our family had lower priority, always on hold, always in the future.

I still walk through those rooms in my mind. Plastered lath walls divided the length into three; a kitchen with a doorway into the "front room," where a wider doorway led into the bedroom.

A small entrance porch housed the DeLaval cream separator in warm months. We moved the separator into the kitchen, in the corner behind the door, for winter. In another kitchen corner a Singer sewing machine sat below the wall telephone whose long black mouthpiece served as a coat rack. When the phone rang two long rings, our code on the party line, we lifted the coats and jackets onto the sewing machine. A third kitchen corner had a hand pump over a sink whose drain emptied into a galvanized pail. We felt privileged because, although we had to carry water out, we did not have to carry it in from outside as was common in the community. The fourth kitchen corner housed a small pantry with a curtain for a door.

A kitchen cabinet with its pull-out enameled workspace filled the wall between the pantry and sink. That cabinet held, among other things, a built-in flour bin with sifter, enough mismatched dishes to serve our family, the cod liver oil children forced down all winter, and a magnificent cut glass bowl that had been a wedding gift to my parents. A kerosene lamp sat on a rectangular oak table, pushed up against the kitchen's east wall; beside it were backless benches, our gathering space for meals. Three girls sat on one side; three boys on the other. My dad sat at one short end, my younger sister on the windowsill at the other with her feet resting on one of the benches. My mother perched by the cabinet corner. The cook stove, with its warming ovens and water reservoir, took up the last wall. We toasted bread on the iron cook top and heated bags of salt in its oven to warm icy sheets on wintry nights. A woodbox sat behind the stove, like another hungry mouth waiting to be filled.

Beyond the kitchen, the front room had a square silver-colored heating stove, a storage cupboard, a round pedestal table holding another kerosene lamp, mismatched chairs around the table, the youngest child's white iron crib, one dresser and mirror, and my parent's double bed. Cardboard boxes under the bed and a handmade wooden box painted bright orange provided additional storage.

A clothes rod spanned the doorway between the front room and the bedroom; on it hung the family's entire wardrobe. Clothes were pushed aside at one edge for a space to walk through. The bed for my three older brothers was to the right, the bed I shared with my two sisters on the left, between them a dresser. There was just enough room at the end of each bed for a stack of old magazines and catalogs, precious material for reading or cutting up to make paper dolls. For most of my growing years my oldest sister worked in the big city, so the family at home numbered only nine.

Those were hard times, with grasshopper infestations, foreclosures, and acute shortages of hay and grain. But for children, protected from these grim realities, life was good. Fall and spring were times of eagerness for school to start and eagerness for school to end. Summer days brought glorious barefoot freedom swimming in mud puddles, picking wild berries, swinging on the hay rope, and playing house with cardboard boxes and old clothes stored in the granary.

Close quarters with no private spaces could be tinder for tension. But from early fall we children knew we must keep on our toes. Santa was watching! We found plenty to behave for in the Montgomery Ward and Sears-Roebuck Christmas catalogs. Most likely anything in our stocking beyond an orange and a color book would be something practical. A dress. Long underwear, fleecy on the inside, to wear with long brown stockings that had no darning in the toe. But we dared to dream. A truck, a doll, or the set of doll-sized silverware in its cardboard case with a brown herringbone-checked outside and a pink lining with elastic to hold the tiny knives in place. I had that page of the wish book nearly worn out! We waited and watched for packages to appear under the bed or on top of the cupboard.

Closer to Christmas the entire community gathered at our one-room school for our program. Parents sat in rows of desks screwed to long boards. A humming gasoline lantern hanging high by the front blackboards gave a whiter, brighter light than our kerosene lamps at home. Faded green muslin sheets, stored from year to year in a cupboard in the library across from the cloakroom, were hung on a wire across the front of the school-room. Our small gathering of students waited nervously behind the curtains for the program to begin. At some point my uncle slipped out to dress in a red suit and appear with a gunnysack of candy treats and a hearty ho, ho, ho when the final applause died away.

He handed out little brown bags filled with ribbon candies, and candies like lovely Venetian beads, bright on the outside with poinsettias or candy canes in the white center. What magician could make those, I wondered? Others, in an array of pastel colors, had a thin coating over a fruit, or, if you were lucky, a chocolate filling. There were the ones we called haystacks, chocolate mounds, some pink inside and some white!

Before the evening ended, traditional Finnish tarts, a pinwheel pastry with a prune filling, were served. Each family made the same thing — only they were never really the same. Like the chairs at the three bears' house, some were too large and some were too small. But always, my mother's were just right!

On Christmas Eve our tree must have filled every inch of open space in the front room. Yet, I don't remember being crowded. I don't remember what decorations we used, but I do remember the magic. My dad sat ready with a pail of water as my mother lit the candles in tin holders clipped onto the branches. A dimly lit room, the soft glow from the candles, the aroma of the freshly cut spruce — that is the evening I remember.

At bedtime we hung long brown stockings and hand-knit wool socks on a clothesline strung from corner to corner across the kitchen. Santa left whatever gifts were possible each year. Always an orange, usually a color book, and one year, doll-sized silverware in a cardboard case with brown herringbone-checked paper outside and a pink lining.

The Bells of Karstula

Grieving in silence among strangers, my sorrow mirrored the gloom of the approaching evening. I was scarcely aware of the passing landscape as the bus traveled through the wooded countryside that bleak October afternoon of 1953.

Five months earlier I had arrived by ship in the bustling, flower-filled harbor market of Helsinki, Finland, lugging a suitcase and a bulging leather shoulder bag that cradled a Finnish-English dictionary, a camera with film and flashbulbs for my entire stay, and my passport and immunization record. One of four exchange program delegates, I would share the lives of four farm families that summer and fall.

I received personal travel time at the end of the home stays, and on a happier day chose to visit my immigrant-grandmother's hometown, Karstula, to stay for two nights at the home of Eino Palovesi, a member of the Finnish Parliament who lived nearby.

By October the sun, so bright in June, was a colorless orb low in the sky, foreshadowing the dark Nordic winter. The joyous day on which I had arrived contrasted sharply with the dreary, dismal days nearing my departure. Home seemed near; my leave of Finland was underway, yet home seemed unbearably distant. A week ago I had received a troubling message from my sister. My grandmother, who lived with my parents, was in failing health. The doctor caring for her told the family, "You must write to Marlene and tell her that Grandma will not be here when she gets home."

Tragically, I then received a telegram bearing these words: "JOHNNY KILLED. CAR ACCIDENT. FINISH YOUR TRIP. DAD." Johnny was my oldest brother.

Unexpectedly losing a brother only nine years older than I caused grief such as I had never imagined. Grandma's death would be more in keeping with the natural order of things.

I did not know that as my sister's letter reached me, a letter I had written home arrived in Minnesota. My sister read it, then went into my grandmother's bedroom and said quietly, "Marlene is going to visit Karstula." Grandma, too weak to speak, must have understood that news, for she turned in her bed and, alone with her thoughts, stared silently at the wall.

My troubled reflections were interrupted when the bus driver announced a brief coffee stop at Karstula. With scarcely another person around the café that served as the bus station, I walked across the parking lot and up the sloping street toward the ocher, orthodox-style church. Its separate bell tower, silhouetted in fading light of the shortened autumn days, dominated the highest point in town. As I drew near, a melodic sound met me, the pealing of church bells. I knew, from a magazine article, that the bells of this church were prized for their superb quality.

I glanced at my watch. Close to the hour, I assumed it was the usual time for the bells to ring. I could not know the significance of the event then, but I knew I would remember this beautiful tone and carry that memory home.

I turned from the church, walked back to board the bus, and mentally prepared for a draining evening ahead. A short distance from town I was dropped at my host's home.

The next afternoon Mr. Palovesi took me to visit the church; another man, perhaps the custodian, perhaps not, met us there. As we entered, I ran my hand lightly over the ornate brass hardware on the inner door. Reading my thoughts, the men volunteered that it was indeed the same handle my grandmother would have touched. Certain things had not changed, I realized.

We entered the sanctuary and I moved about the church, seeking solace in the painting of Jesus in the fishing boat calming the waters, admiring the gilded circular canopy over the elevated pedestal pulpit, noting the sheen of the red velvet cushions around the semi-circular altar. I heard the men, neither of whom spoke English, conversing about the repairs taking place. Extensive restoration was underway, as the building was a century old that year. Our guide remarked that it was regrettable that the bells were not working so that I could hear them. Puzzled, I blurted in Finnish, "Mutta mina kuulin kellot!" "But I heard the bells!"

Not understanding, he repeated that it was regrettable that the bells were not working. Again I insisted I had heard them the previous afternoon. My host, still believing I misunderstood, was about to explain again, when the guide asked what time I had heard the bells. Visibly moved, he related haltingly that the afternoon before he had sensed an urgency to try one last time to make a repair. He had gone to the church, climbed the ladder inside the tower, and had rung the bells by hand just as I started toward the church. In the stunned silence that followed, each of us recognized an extraordinary happening.

That evening a gathering in my honor was arranged at the church. There the story was told; how the bells, silent for years, rang during those few minutes a granddaughter from America walked toward her grandmother's childhood church. It is said that Finnish people do not show emotion readily, but that night many wept openly, hugging me and saying, "You are like a relative." And, "It is as though your grandmother has come back."

I arrived home in November with this remarkable story to tell my grandmother who, from the day of my letter's arrival, astounded her doctor and her family, and gained strength to live another six years.

I gave an account of my exchange experiences to more than 200 audiences in schools and clubs throughout Minnesota under the auspices of the University of Minnesota Extension Service, but never the story of the bells of Karstula. I told that story only in my parents' home. On many weekend visits my father asked me to show my slides. The narrative of my church visit was what he wanted to hear again and again.

One evening in the darkened dining room, I glanced at my grandmother. Years later I yet see the tears glistening in her eyes in the beam cast by my slide projector as we relived the miracle that brought the past into the present, the far and near together, the day the broken bells of Karstula rang.

Dollar Bay, 1954

Sunday March 28, 1954, my twenty-second birthday. Skies were clear outside Minneapolis-St. Paul International airport as I waited to board the 8:25 a.m. North Central flight to Duluth-Superior with a short connecting hop to Ironwood, Michigan. I looked forward to seeing the upper Peninsula, an area I knew little about although it was there my family's immigrant history began.

A travel-scarred suitcase had been my home base for nearly a year, but no luggage was necessary for this one-day round trip. A bulky leather purse carried the only essential paraphernalia — a box of 35mm slides taken during a summer and autumn with Finnish farm families under the International Farm Youth Exchange program.

After returning in November I'd traveled for the University of Minnesota Agricultural Extension Service, speaking about those experiences. County Agents delivered me from town-to-town, audience-to-audience, toting their 35mm projector and screen and my carousel of slides. The experience was gratifying, the schedule grueling.

I spoke up to three and four times a day, a total of 113 speeches to 4-H and Rural Youth clubs, PTAs, elementary and high schools, travel clubs, garden clubs, study clubs, Rotary and Lions clubs, Farm Bureaus, Lutheran men's night, Methodist family night, the Finnish Ladies of Kaleva, and the national farm safety winners at 4-H Club Congress in Chicago. Audience size ranged from 15 adults at the Rural Norseland 4-H Leaders Institute to 600 students at St. Cloud State Teachers College to 2,500 patrons at the Land O'Lakes annual meeting in Minneapolis.

After that appearance, Land O'Lakes requested another — to dedicate their Copper Country Cheese Co-op affiliate in Dollar Bay, Michigan. As Land O'Lakes was a sponsor of our exchange program, of course the answer was yes.

Their next request was that I deliver the speech in Finnish. I surmised that many in the audience would be immigrant and first-generation Americans who used Finnish as their first language. But without hesitation, I again said yes.

I don't know where the audacity came from. As a child, I had never spoken the language, although it existed side-by-side with English in our home. While preparing for the trip I learned phrases from language records, and could rattle off, "This is a picture of a living room. In the living room are a father, mother, grandfather, and grandmother." When living with host families, my Finnish-English and English-Finnish dictionaries were never far from reach. A painfully stilted and grammatically flawed vocabulary succeeded in answering questions and communicating what needed to be said.

By 1953, the fifth year of our exchange program, it had become traditional for a returning delegate to wear clothing representative of their host country when giving speeches. I wore the national dress of my grandmother's home province — a knife-pleated, colorfully striped wool skirt, a silver pin at the neckline of a long-sleeved white linen blouse with hand-tied lace trim at the neck and wrists, a fitted bodice laced through silver eyelets, and, instead of a cap, a ribbon in my hair to indicate that I was unmarried.

Flying in the 1950s, now referred to as the Golden Age of Air Travel, was perceived to be glamorous. People wore fashionable outfits — suits, dresses, ties, hats and gloves, high heels and hose. I wore my national dress, completely obvlivious to the reaction of other passengers on that 21-seat Douglas DC3, or the very attentive male cabin steward.

A Land O'Lakes field representative met the plane at Ironwood, 133 miles and two hours of conversation from Dollar Bay, a small community located where the Keweenaw Peninsula juts into Lake Superior. This man was not Finnish, but with wit and whimsy demonstrated his respect for the close-knit culture of the Finnish people. We bonded quickly. I told him the very little I knew then about my Upper Peninsula connections, that my mother was born in Calumet and that my great-grandfather had perished in a copper mining disaster.

He explained the history of the Copper Country Dairy, established in the late 1930s when incorporation papers were signed by nine dairy farmers, all Finnish. In 1952 Land O'Lakes submitted a project proposal for a new cheese plant. In time he was summoned to the board meeting where a vote would determine the outcome of that proposal. Coming prepared with facts, figures, and supporting materials, he felt ready to answer any and all questions.

Puzzled, he then sat in silence while the board meeting was conducted entirely in Finnish; not one question was directed to him. Finally, after a thorough examination of documents and much lengthy discussion, none of which the field representative understood, the chairperson stood, reached out his hand, and with a smile and a handshake said in English, "Well Bob, you got the job."

On this cold and icy March day, cars filled designated parking spaces and lined both sides of the narrow street in front of the low, brick-faced building at the edge of town. A green sign with yellow and white letters identified this as the "Copper Country Cheese Co-op, Inc."

Inside, we were directed to a large space with concrete block walls. A temporary stage area was established at one end. Here a lectern bearing the logo CCC (Copper Country Cooperative) was flanked with gigantic bouquets of orange gladiolas, yellow jonquils, purple iris, and white chrysanthemums, a message of congratulations affixed to each. The darkness of the room went well with the somber faces of male executives milling around in dark suits, white shirts, and subdued ties.

I slipped my slides into a waiting carousel as the rows of folding chairs began to fill with a very Finnish-looking audience of

600. Having spoken to similar groups on the Minnesota Iron Range, I realized how close to the Old Country they were. I sensed many hearts would ache as they saw images of lakes and fields and pines, and heard about the efforts of a war-torn nation to rebuild after devastating years of war.

I told about the families who opened their homes to a stranger and allowed her to become family. I delivered the message of our program, that peace was possible through understanding.

That belief seems embarrassingly naive today as our world whirls faster and faster toward devastation and the survival of the planet itself is at stake. Our program participants were ages 20 to 30. Today activists on the world stage are often teenagers, like Swedish 16-year-old Greta Thunberg, whose very childhood has been stripped away. We must ask, has our time run out?

The last time I visited Dollar Bay, the cheese plant was abandoned and partially dismanted. The economy of the Upper Peninsula changed drastically and in 1977 the Cooperative began experiencing financial problems. By 1984 it could no longer pay its producers, many quit, and Copper Country Cooperative was forced to end operations September 24, 1985.

From the remains of the building I chose a memento, one chipped and broken brick.

The Cut Glass Bowl

Dishes are stored in the kitchen cupboard of my childhood memories — the oversized black pan in which Mother baked the three-day rolls of family fame, the crazed white oval platter, the enamel pot where my mother brewed tea leaves at the back of the wood stove. Nearby, the sides of white dishpans are splotched with blackness where the enamel is chipped; the gray coffee pot stands ready to boil coffee for District 51 PTA meetings, Christmas programs, and picnics.

Our kitchen, as others of that era, had no wall-mounted cupboards. A freestanding cabinet doled out dinnerware — plates often mismatched, cup handles occasionally missing, chips never taken seriously. A pullout work shelf over the silverware and utensil drawers divided the lower storage compartment from the two main sections of the top. Behind the left door was a flour bin with a built-in sifter; behind the right, our entire stock of plates, cups, saucers, and glassware. Important letters, none more important than those from sons serving in the Pacific, a Marine and two sailors, were filed next to the plates, giving assurance of the boys' safety a short time before. The top center space held larger dishes and smaller bric-a-brac. Here my mother kept the cut glass bowl.

Intricately cut with prisms and patterns, perhaps six or seven inches across, the bowl broadcast a ringing tone when snapped with a finger — the mark of fine glass, my mother told us. Our tiny house offered no place for it to be displayed and admired. Never was it used for a serving bowl; it was too special for that. It was the Cut Glass Bowl. There was an aura to those words.

As long as I can remember, the bowl had been there in the cupboard, a wedding gift to my parents. That much my younger sister and I recall, but we never asked from whom the gift was received. Now the last of eight surviving children, we pool our memories and pose the question. But it is too late; neither of us has an answer.

Sometimes, as we washed and dried supper dishes by kerosene lamplight, a wood fire crackling in our cook stove, Mother told us about working in Duluth as a domestic when she was yet a young girl. She spoke of learning the "proper" way to run a home, the rules for keeping a kosher kitchen, the etiquette of serving guests in Duluth mansions.

Though these stories could have sounded like "Cinderella Visits the Palace," they did not. Through disappointments, difficulties, and extreme poverty of the Great Depression, my mother retained her self-esteem. She felt no less worthy for having such a humble home, and so, for the most part, neither did we. It might have been on such evenings that we took out the cut glass bowl to look at and admire, to snap it carefully and hear its clear ringing tone.

The Single Treasure

A week after our wedding we moved into our brand-new 8-foot-wide, 41-foot-long trailer home in Lowry Grove Mobile Manor, Northeast Minneapolis. Outside and inside were splashes of the trendy color of the 50s, pink. The longest in the park — I deemed it perfect!

We'd flown in the dealer's private plane from Montevideo, Minnesota, to Marathon, Wisconsin, to place our order, now installed in Space C-3, second row from the back (rows A and B had been combined as trailers became longer), third space in from Stinson Boulevard. That first fall and winter, involved with university coursework and part-time jobs, we spent little time with neighbors, although we had established a wave-from-the-window friendship with Ellen Frederickson, the little girl next door.

But almost immediately, Jerry Boss in Space C-4 became central to our marriage lore. He appeared the day after we moved in and announced with great bluster that he was moving into a 10-foot-wide 50-footer, the first 10-wide in the park. So much for our short reign as the Joneses of Lowry Grove!

Handsome in a cocky sort of way, Jerry looked as though he could be Italian, and in all seriousness he thought he must be because he "liked spaghetti so much." He could not be certain, for he was abandoned as an infant on the steps of a Catholic church and raised in foster homes. The closest he had to a mother was the saintly woman who kept him through his teen years — Jerry remained in touch with her during the time we knew him.

Toni Boss was attractive, industrious, authentic — in some ways far different from Jerry. While Jerry was experienced in city ways, Toni, nee Antoinette Fisher, was raised in rural Onamia, Minnesota. One of Jerry's favorite lines referenced the General Motors logo when he bragged he had a wife with a "Body by Fisher."

Jerry worked at various jobs during the nearly five years we knew him. We cannot remember their sequence or duration, but we gained the most conversational fodder from his stint as a night-shift trash collector. He frequently brought us sacks of sweets from the bakery that was one of the company's clients. We suspected that was not a legitimate benefit of the job. Jerry appeared at our door with rolls one Saturday morning, assuring a disconcerted houseguest that the rolls were edible because he'd brushed off any debris. Later we managed to assure her that Jerry was fastidious about cleanliness, that he'd almost certainly heisted them from a baking sheet, and that we should enjoy the treats.

Jerry was addicted to purchasing, practicality being of no concern. Occasionally he called on Harlan to help carry the top-of-the-line Shopsmith down three steps from the attached storage shed to the yard so Jerry could saw a board or, more likely, just admire his saw and its attachments. He glowed with pride over his used baby-blue Cadillac. A salesperson's delight, he'd demand, "Give me the best you got. I don't want no junk!"

We recognized Jerry's ruses to ward off bill collectors and caught on to why the Cadillac would on occasion be parked on A-row, making it less obvious that he was home. Once three bill collectors were gathered at Jerry's door when Jerry, savvy enough to have parked on Stinson Boulevard, walked jauntily past our front windows. He strode into his space, and seeing the other men, joined the line and asked, "Ain't that guy home yet?" He waited with them a short time, then, feigning impatience, announced he had better things to do, left, and returned when the coast was clear.

Over time our circle of friends widened a bit, but we basically kept it to a small and memorable assortment. We enjoyed the South Dakota decency of the Hornings, Bill and Rita, who lived in Space C-6. And we were greatly entertained by the antics of Gene and Dee Morstad across the street in D-row.

Gene was an English major in no hurry to graduate; Dee had been Pea Soup Queen of Somerset, Wisconsin. Born on a houseboat in tri-state waters of the Mississippi, Dee seemed destined to live an unusual life. Her father, an author of children's books, imposed unique theories about child rearing on to his family. He built the family home around a living tree and installed the kitchen sink lower than standard height; he considered dishwashing the children's responsibility. Although the mother was burdened by this sink oddity, the children found the tree convenient for hanging dishtowels to dry.

The Morstads shared details of their financial shortages freely. We rejoiced with them when they had saved enough money for a new mattress. On delivery day we gathered in their yard as Gene began to cut away the paperboard carton. Ignoring instructions, he cut a lengthwise swatch down the center of the package with a utility knife and with a flourish pulled away the wrapping. To everyone's horror, he had slashed through the mattress cover and into the foam.

With a surplus of free time during the summer, Toni, Rita, and I began frequenting the opening morning of sales at M.F. Banks, a salvage company located in an imposing five-story building in Northeast Minneapolis. Banks specialized in buying surplus goods and selling at drastic reductions. A chalkboard in the store announced future sales — household goods, linens, giftware, tools, shoes, women's clothing, men's clothing, baby clothing. None of us had a baby, nor was there anything else we actually needed, but it was the joy of the hunt, the competition against other Banks-addicts like us, and ultimately the camaraderie of individuals not in our usual circle.

Rita's husband, Bill, taught at DeLaSalle High School but for the summer worked the night shift at the Gluek brewery. As a favor, he offered to take his lunch break at the top of the steps at Banks, going there at 4 a.m. on sale mornings. Spreading a

blanket to mark our territory, he waited until we arrived some-
where before 5 with a thermos of coffee and enough treats to
carry us until the 8 a.m. opening click of the front door.

I don't remember precisely what we talked about in those pre-
dawn hours, but I remember the changing mood as a sleeping
city awoke. Traffic picked up. Lights went on in dark buildings.
Other shoppers arrived; we knew a few by sight, but none by
name. There was absolute honor among Banks shoppers. No one
sneaked ahead in line. No one grouched because we had cap-
tured the space at the top of the stairs where we could sit, sip
coffee, and lounge comfortably while they stood on the lower
steps and the sidewalk.

I salvaged a chance aphorism one morning, when over the
sleepy murmur of the crowd, an unseen woman declared, "Ethel
ain't got no taste!"

Harlan and I use that expression now and then, thankful to
an unknown Ethel and the bequeathed expression, the single
treasure that remains of all I ever brought home from Banks.

Did I Teach Too Long?

I've thought of Alma often since I retired from teaching. Plain. Childless. The spinster country school marm. She, this teacher of wisdom, met and married my dad's brother and, in the days before I can remember, became a possessive. We called her Emil's Alma.

Emil, my rough-hewn, bib-overalled farmer uncle, knew little of communing with children. But Emil's Alma, this childless aunt, played with us — my brother, my sisters, and me. We tagged along with our father on visits and occasionally were brought to spend a day, or an afternoon. We'd be invited into the "front room," where intriguing treasures lay. I especially remember the jigsaw puzzles — wooden, not the cardboard we see today. We'd put a jumble of pieces on the table and, as taught, sort the edge pieces and begin to work. Not soon, for the puzzles were very large, but after trial and struggle, a beautiful picture emerged.

I wish I could say that those days were pure pleasure, but I recall that the play felt structured, with always a tinge of pressure. Bashful child that I was, I felt on edge. Would we do something wrong? Would we somehow misbehave and not know why?

Oh, how little we comprehended about her!

Now, years later, I place a jumble of memories on the table. I believe that if I look back and struggle once again, I may, after a time, piece together a picture of my Aunt Alma. But so many pieces of who and what she was are missing. I have told you the most obvious, the edge pieces. Plain, childless, the spinster school marm who met and married my dad's brother. This teacher of wisdom who played with us.

When I was seventeen and starting college, only Emil's Alma offered vocational advice. In my world, little advice was given, for a girl's career choices amounted to little more than staying in town and clerking at the co-op store, leaving town on the Greyhound bus the morning after graduation, or teaching. Although secretly I wished to be an archaeologist, I would teach.

This decision was accepted without comment by other relatives who inquired. But Emil's Alma made this plea to me: "Marlene, don't teach too long. If you do, you will always want to correct everyone and everything around you."

I wonder what prompted those plain words spoken years ago. Were they an admission of what she knew about herself? Did she long to correct our shy, bashful ways? Was she saying she had taught too long?

My life unfolded. I had a career in teaching, a career correcting things around me. At nineteen, armed with an Associate in Education degree and a box of red correcting pencils, I stood before my first classroom, thirty-nine seven-year-olds from a small town and the adjoining consolidated area. The lines of responsibility were clear. Parents were in charge of parenting; I was in charge of the three Rs.

Routine ruled. Students passed workbooks forward from the back of the row, placing theirs on top of the pile. The next day, after I'd emblazoned the pages with a red star or with red check marks, signaling "correct the error here," the workbooks were returned in the same order, again making their way from the back of the row to the front student.

Communication from parents consisted of a signature on the returned report card, a note after an absence, and a customary Christmas gift. School doors were left unlocked all day; we were not afraid of intruding strangers. I had no classroom or file drawer keys. My grade book lay in the center desk drawer and my purse at the bottom of the narrow coat closet by the door. On any Saturday, most of the elementary teachers were at school, sharpening their correcting pencils and updating their bulletin board displays of "Good Work." Teachers were readily recognized in the community; their pictures were published in the paper each fall. While keenly observed, teachers remained separate, a congregation of their own.

At a later, but still early, stage of my teaching career, I was equipped with a bachelor's degree and employed by a suburban district. We held parent-teacher conferences. Interaction between a child's home and school was greater. But, in general, life was simple, and routine still ruled.

I applied newly acquired knowledge about meeting the individual learning needs of children. A fourth grader presented a research paper about an animal of his choice. In its entirety, his report said, "A greatly enlarged photograph of the North American Bark Beetle." He told me he had composed it himself. He clung to his story, even as I showed him those exact words under an illustration in the classroom encyclopedia. I treated him gently.

Years later, in a different suburban school, a fifth grader awoke and readied himself for school because his mother did not. He was tardy so often his classmates tended to ignore him and treat him like The-Boy-Who-Isn't-Here. I sensed his need to feel needed, and forged first a deal with the custodian, then a deal with the child. If he arrived at school early, he would be allowed to put up the school flag. For a time, at least, he became The-Boy-To-Be-Envied.

In time, the routines of my early teaching became impossible to maintain. My correcting pens were often inadequate in situations I now faced, as when a troubled student called for help in a note covered with violent images drawn in dark, angry pencil strokes. The tortured images bore his name. The school psychologist directed a plan of action.

In a voice devoid of emotion, a ten-year-old confided: "My dad broke my little sister's arm last night." Legally, I had to make that sad report to the proper authorities.

Large for his age, a newly enrolled fifth grader suffered the double humiliation of our having to order a larger desk for him and of his knowing that classmates knew his father was in prison. When he proposed to build an atomic bomb for his science fair project, his progress reports were consistent: "I need just one more ingredient." Was this an ego-preservation attempt or a veiled notice to classmates to not mess with him? Thirty years and more had passed since I'd entered a classroom. The world and teaching were no longer simple.

Over the years we amused each other, angered each other, inspired each other, all in the process of teaching each other. A kindergarten student decreed fervently, "You are the best science teacher I ever had," then added, "Well, you are the only science teacher I ever had." An excited third grader struggled with two grocery bags of food he brought for the food drive. Asked if his mother knew, he avoided a direct reply. "I just took the things I don't like." When I attempted to impress upon the class how hard nest-building must be for birds, a seven-year-old said wistfully, "It would be worth it though, if you could fly."

Students learned about life when the classroom pet population gave us large litters. They learned about death when burying beloved hamsters wrapped in soft cloths and placed in caskets my husband had made and they had decorated with messages reading "Rest in peace" and "We will always remember you."

I have memories of a Polish refugee — in those years called Displaced Persons — who caught on to reading just when it was time to go outside for recess. Coming back to the room, he did not stop to take off his jacket, but rushed to check the words in the book and shouted jubilantly, "I can still read it, Miss Mattila! I can still read it!"

I remember the little girl from a large family that had money for a little beyond the necessities. She gave me a freshly ironed but frayed floral handkerchief. Given with love, it was the perfect Christmas gift.

And the girl who invented an "energy-saver" — a tracing of her tiny brown hand on pure white tag board stapled to a short stick. Now she could raise the stick instead of her entire arm to volunteer an answer in class. She gave me her invention at the end of the year and it, along with the frayed floral handkerchief, is in my box of teaching treasures. In my heart, I store memories of these students and scores of others — along with the words of caution from Emil's Alma as I prepared to become a teacher.

Perhaps by digging into old memories to piece together a picture of my aunt, I am finally doing archaeology, the study of antiquity, the dream unattainable in my childhood. And I wonder, did I fail to heed her advice?

I will let someone else decide. I choose to remember those times when I knew I'd reached a child. At those times I had not been there too long.

Go to Kuusamo

While Grandma learned to speak English well, my grandfather mastered but a few words. Conversations, if they could be considered such, between Grandpa and the youngest of his grandchildren consisted of a few bantering phrases delivered with a teasing smile. "Go to Kuusamo," Grandpa would say. We parroted back, "No, *you* go to Kuusamo!" Kuusamo was the Finnish town of Grandpa's birth.

I knew little about this quiet man from Kuusamo. I knew he cut the logs and built the schoolhouse that became the Wadena County Red Eye Township Hall. I did not know he served on the first township board and was treasurer for many years.

I knew he emigrated as a young man. I did not know he came with his brother with whom he ran a blacksmith shop, building wheels for farm wagons, runners for sleighs, and plow parts for farmers.

Neither did I know he was of Sami background.

World War II raged. In country school we sang anti-Axis songs with hateful lyrics, collected scrap and toothpaste tubes for the war effort, cleaned our plates in the name of patriotism. Less vivid are memories of mailing packages to Finland to ease that nation's suffering.

Grandpa did not live to see the war's end. He died in 1944, at age 91; I was 12. His unmarried son kept the farm going; Grandma relied more and more upon our family for household help. My sisters and I, self-taught drivers without licenses, regularly drove the four miles in our standard-shift Ford to bring Grandma and her laundry to wash in our sauna.

At St. Cloud State Teachers College I joined the Student Project for Amity among Nations, not because I could afford study abroad, but because I identified with others persuaded of the importance of international understanding.

In 1953 I applied for and was chosen for the International Farm Youth Exchange, begun by 4-H alumni convinced that understanding others, the key to world peace, could be achieved through exchanges of young people.

For six months I lived with Finnish families, taken into their hearts and homes, cutting hay by hand in the sunny days of June, harvesting mushrooms in leafy forests in summer, picking potatoes in cold rains of October. Interspersed between home stays was travel with national 4-H staff to camps and exhibitions.

At war-torn Rovaniemi, where "not one stone had remained upon another," we visited garden plots and toured the agricultural station to observe grass and grain experiments. The consequences of what humans had done to this land were vivid: war and peace — death and life — destruction and reconstruction."

I married; we raised two daughters. I joined the state 4-H staff, conducting the inbound phase of international exchanges at the University of Minnesota while earning a master's degree in intercultural communication.

Travel remained a priority. Viewing the barren Norwegian seacoast with my husband from the windows of the Hurtigruten coastal boat, I felt I was retracing dangerous waters of an ancestral habitat. Traveling by bus on a winding road from Hammerfest, a rocky hillside on one side, a fjord on the other, we stopped to wait as reindeer, which have the right of way, decided at their leisure to let mere humans pass. Soon the only passengers, we looked upon snow-covered ground and shrubs; there were no trees. In the hotel dining room in Karasjok, our waitress wore Sami dress. Daughter of a reindeer herder, she shared plans for a yearlong high school graduation trip around the world before college.

In art galleries and museums we viewed objects of incredible beauty. Surrounded by the breathtaking architecture of Sami Parliament buildings at Inari and Karasjok, aware of the legislative accomplishments made on their own behalf, we marveled that Sami could once have been regarded as uncivilized, backward people.

Ultimately, exploration into my family roots brought an overnight stay in Kuusamo, my first visit to Grandpa's parish. I searched without success for our family name on tombstones in the churchyard and purchased a birch drinking-cup at the village market.

Three years later we returned. Our innkeeper, remembering our connection to the town, urged me to call his friend who had researched the history of Kuusamo. Reluctantly, I accepted this thoughtfulness, giving the only information I had, Grandpa's name and my email address.

On returning home an email awaited: "I think I have found your August Mattila." There was my genealogy traced back to a birth in 1668 (see page 111), and the statement, "Antti Sarvi-Sarve was Samish, but then this family left the Sami lifeway and began to farm." The hotelkeeper's friend, Veikko Väätäinen, deceased within months of our encounter, was Finland's foremost genealogist.

How enriched my life has been from having followed Grandpa's childhood dictate, "Go to Kuusamo."

Confessions of a Bowerbird

As a child I gathered stones from roadsides, shells from lakeshores, and fungi and other oddments in nature, as comes naturally to children. After discovering *The Early Cavemen* and *The Later Cavemen* books in our country school library, I began to hunt with purpose, scouring fields and roadsides for evidence these early people had lived on our farm. A grey stone shaped like the wing of the county snowplow caught my eye. I believed it might be an ancient scraping tool. Perhaps it was; no expert has looked at it. It is stored away in an old mauve and silver, foil-covered, candy box.

My stone collection grew and grew. My dad gave me a wooden box, perhaps four feet long, 18 inches across, in which I stored my treasure under the poplar grove at the edge of the yard. In quiet moments I sorted my stones over and over. I once overheard my older sister say to a visitor, ". . . and she knows every one of them by name!" I painfully remember coming home from school to discover that the workmen pouring the basement for our new house had added my stones to the mix! At least I know where they are today.

Years later, while researching nest-building techniques for a second-grade science unit, I learned of the bowerbird found in Australia, New Guinea, and nearby islands. In its mating behavior, the bowerbird builds structures or overarching bowers and decorates them with brightly colored objects — foil, stones, shells, colored glass, insulated wire, feathers, discarded plastic, lichen and other plant materials — sorting and arranging them by type or favorite color.

I realized then that I had been born a bowerbird! Our home is filled with collections. They no longer fit in foil candy boxes or four-foot wooden boxes, and they are not referred to as collections, but as accessories. They move from place to place or in and out of storage, to be arranged and displayed on mantels, tables, and shelves.

Of our two daughters, one does not wish to own these treasures, except for the cold-chisel sculpture of birds and flowers, signed LOUISJLISTE, that I purchased in The Virgin Islands. Our younger daughter, aware of the stories behind many of these objects, reminds me, "Mom, be sure you write down where all these things are from."

This then is an introduction to the stories behind my acquired treasures, these enticements in our bower. Starting with the items in the old type case on one wall in our bedroom I will relate, as well as I am able, the stories behind them.

Space 1: Two miniatures, from garage or estate sales

The Great Buddha (material unknown) is a miniature of the bronze statue that stands on the grounds of Kotokuin Temple in Kamakura, Japan.

Tom and Toshiko Okamoto, of Kawasaki, hosted me from July 22 to August 22, 1982, when I chaperoned the Minnesota 4-H/Labo International Exchange Program delegation to Japan. Toshi arranged for me to visit the temple and to meet with the governor of the prefecture in which it is located.

The Buddha, 43.8 feet tall and dating to 1252, is believed cast from melted Chinese coins, and then plated with gold. Because it has stood in the open air since the temple building was destroyed by a tsunami in 1492, only traces of gold leaf remain on the right cheek.

My netsuke is of carved bone or ivory. Traditional Japanese kimonos had no pockets, but men needed a place to store money, pipes, tobacco, seals, medicine or other personal belongings. The solution was to place such objects in containers hung by cords from their sashes (obi) that were closed with sliding beads on cords. The fastener that secured the cord was called a netsuke.

74

Netsuke took many forms: people, animals, plants, deities, and mythical creatures. Mine represents Hotei, one of the Seven Gods of Good Fortune in Japanese mythology. The guardian of children and god of popularity, Hotei is a happy, fat, bald man with a curly moustache, always appearing half-naked as his clothes are not large enough to cover his enormous belly.

Space 2: Three carved animals

Wooden moose. This moose was among things Kirstie Hirvensalo of the Maatalouskerholiito (4-H) staff chose for me with money I left in Finland at the end of my IFYE experience in 1953. As our group of four gathered in Helsinki I received the devastating telegram telling me my brother Johnny had died in a car crash in California. Because I was too stunned to think of shopping, Kirstie took over, choosing and then mailing items to me. Also included was the carved wooden wall plaque of a sauna scene and the crystal bowl created and signed by artist Tapio Wirkkala, whom I had met at a 4-H exhibition.

Pipestone turtle. In the months before Harlan and I were married he was headquartered in Lincoln/Lyon Counties prior to enrolling at the U of M. I would be a senior at the U and took a summer job as 4-H agent in Lyon County, headquartered at Marshall. On one of his Sundays off we visited the quarries at the Pipestone National Monument, source of the sacred stone known as catlinite that the Plains tribes used for pipe making. The turtle, a fertility symbol, is one of the biggest sellers in the gift shop.

Hippo. During winter jaunts we discovered a home-away-from-home near the small Oklahoma city of 6,623 residents, Grove. Prior to statehood, this area was part of the Cherokee Nation in Indian Territory. Even with that rich cultural heritage the town was named for a grove of trees standing on its site.

Each time we visited Grove we met interesting people. For example, I needed a new watch battery; the jeweler installed the battery and treated us to a fresh doughnut. I checked out a store with interesting second-hand items in its window and was asked my opinion of the business plan the woman that afternoon planned to present to the rest of the group of women who run it.

We had seen a dilapidated building one block off Grove's main street with cluttered window displays and stock that even when the store was closed (as it was most of the time) spilled out into the tacked-on entryway and onto the sidewalk. The owner had status among antique and second-hand dealers in the area, being responsible for updating and distributing the list of stores in the entire area. One lucky day we saw a light inside.

I have a system for visits to antique or junk stores; I ask for a specific item. That year I was looking for "miniature animals for a friend's collection." Harlan asked about old books and sheet music and was directed upstairs. On descending and describing the rickety condition of the steps and the scene he found upstairs, he advised me not to go up there.

The owner asked me to follow as we squeezed through tiny slots between boxes and cupboards, cautioning me to watch my step. She knew exactly what she had and where it was. I bought the adorable carved hippo; it never made it to my friend's collection.

Space 3: Danish fisherwomen

After my exchange experience in Finland ended, I flew to Copenhagen to join other delegates for travel in Europe before assembling in Paris and sailing to New York City on HMS Queen Elizabeth. These wooden fisherwomen reminded me of the Finnish women found every day, all year around, in the open marketplace in the Helsinki harbor.

Space 4: Ivory carvings

Some of Alaska's best carvers live in the Yupik village of Gambell on Alaska's St. Lawrence Island (population 681 in 2010 census). The island, closer to Russia than to the Alaskan mainland, is thought to be one of the last exposed portions of the land bridge that once joined Asia and the North American continent.

Heading to Sitka on the MV Kennicott, I began conversing with a young Yupik woman taking bone and ivory carvings from Gambell artists to the gift shop in Sitka. Sensing my interest, she said the cost would be less if I purchased from her. I chose these four items: an owl and a seal by Gordon Oozevaseuk, and a seal and a walrus by Robert Apatiki.

Space 5: Ole the Hermit wood carvings

Before Highway 10 was rerouted around Staples, we occasionally stopped at an antique store there. One day I discovered a wood-carving stamped *Ole the Hermit*.

The artist's actual name was Ole A. Olson. Born in Norway in 1882, Ole's family emigrated to the United States when he was one year old, homesteading near Litchville, North Dakota. The family attended North LaMoure Lutheran Church; the children attended rural school.

Ole was the oldest of eight children. Their father died when Ole was 16 and he took over the farm. He served in France in the U.S. military during World War I. In 1921 he married an Irish girl named Hazel and the newlyweds moved in with Ole's mother.

The marriage was not a happy one. Ole's mother and most of the neighborhood women spoke only Norwegian, which Hazel neither spoke nor understood. Hazel was a poor cook and so the couple neither went to social gatherings nor invited friends or relatives to their home.

Hazel died in 1934. In 1942 Ole moved to Valley City, North Dakota, with only his cat, Bertha, for company. He continued to carve and displayed his woodcarvings in the front room of his house — men in ill-fitting clothing, women wearing shawls, people fishing and reading the Bible, biblical personages, an entire donkey ball game.

Despite his name, Ole was far from being a hermit — his guest book listed visitors from Hawaii, Europe, Africa and the Philippines. When a Chicago department store offered a salary to sit and carve while shoppers watched, Ole refused, saying, "What do you think I am? A monkey in a cage?"

Money held no interest for Ole. Hit by a car while crossing the street and advised he was entitled to compensation for pain and suffering, Ole asked only that the doctor and hospital bills be paid. After he died in 1966, many letters in his workbench drawer contained uncashed checks that people had sent in as payment for carvings.

Ole's carvings are still actively sold on the Internet.

Space 6: Three Japanese girls

The three figures of little Japanese girls were a gift on one of my visits to Japan. We had three granddaughters so the figurines were said to represent, by size, Emmy, Heidi, and Molly.

Spaces 7 and 8: Miniature child's tea set

This small tea set cost me 25 cents at a neighbor's estate sale. I have a fondness for such sets, never having anything so delicate in the playhouses we made in the silo or the granary. I also have a larger set, purchased from an antique store for much more money not too many years ago.

Spaces 9 and 10: Three bear fetishes

At a time when we went to Arizona more often, I grew interested in fetishes used by Southwestern tribes for initiation ceremonies, hunting, to cure illness, grant fertility and for personal protection. The Zunis were considered quite skillful, carving not only for their own uses but also for other tribes, tourists, and collectors.

One fetish has a bundle of coral tied to its back, another an arrowhead; these are offerings for favors already received or for those hoped for in the future. The third has an inlaid turquoise "heart line" extending from its mouth. This gives the fetish medicinal power. Or it might also represent a time in Zuni mythology when animals dominated man and the Great Spirit sent a lightning bolt to turn all man-eating animals to stone.

For I Was Hungry…

By that evening the waitress had fallen into the habit of merely pointing us to our usual booth. Our hotel was across the street and, after exhausting hours exploring what the big city and attractions reachable on one-day tours had to offer, we usually had only enough energy to say, "Let's eat at the Chinese place again."

Our booth was the one closest to the entrance, where I had an unobstructed view of the entire dining room while my husband could watch patrons coming or leaving. I ordered sweet and sour chicken served with a vegetable-laden rice. As before, I noted that the servings were far too generous for one person to consume comfortably.

Two women in the next booth were immersed in an animated and prolonged conversation. I wondered about their relationship, perhaps mother-daughter, perhaps aunt-niece.

Meanwhile a man, forty years old or so, came into the restaurant. Immediately a woman bartender came from the adjacent lounge area and indicated that he could not come in there. He stood a moment, then, somewhat unsteadily, made his way to a booth across from us and sat down. The server brought him a glass of ice water and a menu that he glanced over briefly, then put down on the seat beside him.

I studied him briefly and wondered about his circumstances. Long hair spilled out from under a cap pulled low over his forehead. His brown jacket remained zipped tight over his slight body. Bright yellow laces on his scuffed shoes might have been the newest item in his wardrobe.

Although I would guess he was homeless — the city has many homeless people — he did not appear to be dirty. Perhaps he could best be described as appearing hopeless. He sat motionless without looking around, merely sat, as if waiting. The waitress did not approach him to take an order.

By now the women in the next booth had finished eating and the older one asked for a take-out box that she filled with her left-over rice. She put that container in a plastic bag and tied it carefully with a secure knot to make it easy to carry.

Perhaps she noticed the man for the first time as she paid their bill at the cash register. At the point I next saw her, she had walked over to him and handed him her take-out box, saying simply, "God bless you." He nodded a response and put the box on the table without opening it.

I had eaten all my meal that I cared for, so when the waitress offered me a take-out box I impulsively asked, "Could I give the rest of this to that man?"

She double-checked my intent. With a slight motion of her head, she stated, "You want to give this to him." I nodded. She picked up my used fork and my plate with the uneaten sweet and sour chicken with rice, carried it over and placed it in front of him. Without looking around, without a word, he began to dine. At one point he opened and added the container of gifted rice to his plate, squashing down the square mound of cold rice with both hands, and continued to eat.

Then, as silently as he had eaten, the man left the restaurant and returned to the streets.

The Train to Hearst

Rumbling thunder dispatches us on our journey. We are 296 miles from Hearst, Ontario, and the cocoonish sanctuary of our railroad car gives promise of ten hours when weather, good or bad, can but enhance the mood of adventure.

When a family boarded carrying an odorous poodle with a screaming electronic toy, we shuddered. "He doesn't play with it much," the mother volunteered in response to my startled look. The father smoked a cigar before departure, and I feared that aroma, too, might linger. The second passenger car, we speculated, could not be worse. We share this space with two sleeping sweatshirt-clad passengers only.

Incorporated in 1899, intended to reach Hudson Bay but out of money at Hearst, the Algoma Central Railway serves canoeists, fishers, cottagers and tourists seeking a wilderness experience. Scarcely five miles from Sault Ste. Marie we plunge into a lush boreal environment. Branches brush windows and bushes obscure the forest floor. Here, where retreating glaciers scraped bedrock, trees soar to astonishing height with little in which to anchor their roots.

We inch through the spellbinding landscape, hearing the squeak of the platform between cars, the answering groan of the swaying floor beneath us, the clatter of wheels on rails. A mournful four-syllable train whistle announces infrequent road crossings. The forest itself is silent.

At one moment we skirt a wall of rock; at another we look up, down, or out upon a dense woodland. Mile-marker posts allow us to chart progress on our timetable. At Mile 14 we pass through Heyden, the first of several flag stops on the route. No one from Heyden boards the train today.

At Mile 19 we cross an 810-foot-long, 100-foot-high trestle bridge. Our train — an engine, baggage car, and two passenger cars — seems a miniature model and we miniature people, so high are we above the terrain. A higher and longer trestle lies ahead, the 130-foot-high, 1,550-foot-long span over the Montreal River at Mile 92.

At Mile 102 the train begins a descent into Agawa Canyon, terraced with multihued sediment deposited by melting glacial ice. We exit through a 50-foot-wide gap in solid rock. The railroad hugs the overhanging west wall while the river carves its way below the sheer east wall. This is the destination for one-day excursions, but we have the luxury of time, Monday to Friday, and anticipate additional wonders ahead.

Here forests close in, green rickrack wrapping first to one side of the track, then the other. Delicate tamarack, dark-needled spruce, fluttery poplars, tufted pine, and birch unfurling shaggy bark reach toward our window. The sky is blue with building cumulus clouds. Saucer-shaped lakes dot the landscape; room-sized rocks rise from muskeg swamps.

Maroon milkweed sparkles with morning dew, ruby-red raspberries ripen near clusters of pin cherries, yellow black-eyed Susan bloom beside purple phlox. A fern forest grows beside the track, and a bark-bare log floats beside water lilies, green pads forming circles upon the still and stagnant water. A loon dives below a lake surface, its reverie disturbed by the passing train. A startled moose runs along the track, then escapes to the bush.

Passengers are picked up and dropped off, many at open-sided shelters. Two groups haul gear to a pontoon boat, where a canvas top gives only slight protection from a pouring rain. A disparate lot gets off at Mile 165, Hawk Junction, the most popular area for wilderness adventures.

At Miles 210 and 212 we cross the bridges of Squaw Bay and Hoodoo Bay, built on pilings driven into the muskeg. Skeletal trees, now only bare poles, generate jagged reflections in the water. A dead poplar stands upright, saplings encircling it as though performing a maypole dance.

At 7 p.m. we reach our destination, Mile 296, and walk across the train yard to the back door of the Companion Hotel. Hearst is a French-speaking town. The clerk greets us, then, recognizing our tourist status, switches to English. She apologizes. "I am sorry, my restaurant is closed for the civic holiday, but there is a Chinese place. I will check if it is open." We listen in amusement as she calls the Chinese restaurant and converses in French.

This is Hearst, where there is little to do and we do that for three days. We walk the length of this shoestring town on the Trans-Canada Highway, two miles long and four blocks deep, from the Welcome Center on the west to Maki Hardware on the east. In the paint store a man we learn is a teacher relates the town's heritage before the Finns left and the French came. He sends us to the hardware store to meet the only Finnish family left in town and the store's near-eighty-year-old owner. We read at the library; our hotel clerk says no one in town goes to the library to read. "We check out books and take them home with us." There is time for naps and aimless walks and a return to the Chinese restaurant. But soon it is 8:30 Friday morning and time for our return.

The conductor puts our suitcases "in this corner of the baggage car" because "lots of people will get on at Hawk Junction." We innocently settle into our private car. Station names click off in reverse order: Wyborn, Stavert, Coppel, Mead, Horsey.

Most of those "lots of people" who board at Hawk Junction are men sporting vacation beards, as odorous as the pet poodle that, to our displeasure, is again aboard. Four adventurers with one guitar begin to sing in loud twangy voices. I overhear snippets of conversation from four men, one dominating with poorly related tales. His mates teeter at the brink of sleep, feigned, I believe. I surrender to the situation as our train wends its way to Sault Ste. Marie's waiting depot.

Waiting

On the first day of Bon, when Buddhists welcome the spirits of departed ancestors to their household altar, I thought of my young 4-H delegation living for a month in homes throughout Japan. I anticipated that most would attend a community celebration that evening, wearing a gifted or borrowed *yukata*, a summer kimono, and enjoy singing and dancing around a bonfire.

Toshiharu and Toshiko Okamoto hosted me in their home outside of Tokyo. Born into the same generation, although an ocean apart, we bonded, building a friendship not possible for ordinary tourists.

Toshiharu was Buddhist. For him, as for most Japanese, the spiritual significance of Bon had largely faded. But his brother lived on the island where they were raised and had assumed the obligation to care for graves, report to ancestors on family conduct of the past year, and light fires to help the spirits find their way from the other world.

Toshiko, a Christian, respected the Buddhist tenant of continuity between the living and the dead. But that evening, rather than attending a community festival, she took me to the home of a Buddhist friend.

His classic Japanese-style dwelling was exquisite. As we arrived, the outer walls, wooden frames with glass inserts, were open, revealing a room with partitions of sliding wooden panels with rice paper inserts. Rush-covered straw mats covered the floor, and cushions for sitting were spread around the room. The doors of the ornate family altar stood open. Inside I saw a statue of the Buddha, incense burners, and what appeared to be bells. Small bowls of rice, fruit, sweets, and tea were positioned as offerings to the returning spirits.

Toshiko's friend, an old man swathed in an aura of serenity, waited for us outside that room. I was comfortable with the etiquette of bowing. While pleasantries I could not understand were exchanged, I glanced about and realized we stood surrounded by a vast collection of bonsai in a private garden. And then I began to understand the extraordinary experience Toshiko had arranged for me.

We strolled among incredible creations, trees in shallow containers, some more than three hundred years old, their crowns and roots pruned and trained to remain small, mimicking full-sized trees growing in nature.

We did not share a common language — and on that evening it wasn't necessary. After some time, we said goodbye with deep bows of gratitude. Toshiko and I left the garden. Only later did I learn that her friend was a world-famous bonsai master. On that night he was merely a kindly old man waiting to welcome the spirits of his ancestors to his household altar.

CONNECTING
WITH
THE
KEWEENAW

Ancestors of the Keweenaw

This is sacred ground.
—Irene Hepola Bronken

Anna Hepokoski Haara

An older cousin, Mildred Hepola Daubney, remembered our great-grandmother, Anna Haara, widow of Isaac Haara, resting on a kitchen chair in the Hepola farmhouse near Menahga, wrapped in a shawl, headscarf artfully folded over her forehead and tied under her chin, her pipe aglow as she puffed during lapses in the conversation.

Difficulties in Anna's life started shortly after her birth April 18, 1850, at Ii, Finland. That area, Ostrobothnia, traded salted salmon and dried codfish for religious fast days, furs for fashion-conscious nobility, and tar for the shipbuilding industry in the coastal cities. For a time economic prosperity brought a rise in the standard of living.

But in 1853 the Crimean War began. Because Finnish ships sailed under the Russian flag, British and French navies considered them enemies. The British fleet sailed into Oulu, destroyed ships and set fire to stocks of wood products and tar.

Anna was then three years old and her mother, Greta Puurunen Hepokoski, died giving birth to her seventh child. Anna's father, Jacob Hepokoski, remarried three times, only to have three wives and 16 of his 24 children precede him in death.

In the 1860s Finland entered a decade of severe famine. With unrelenting rains, the rivers overflowed and damaged crops. Starvation and disease diminished the population by about ten percent; beggars roamed the countryside. Families subsisted on bread made of tree bark mixed with flour and soup made of reindeer moss in milk.

The spring of 1867 arrived late, once more ending hope of a decent harvest. While her father was among the more successful farmers in the area, tension arose between Anna and her stepmother when she, a compassionate girl of 17, persisted in sharing the family's meager food supplies with those who had nothing at all.

In 1868, the winter she was 18, Anna left home, skiing 400 miles on frozen rivers to Vadsø, Norway, on the Varanger Fjord. There she met and in 1869 married Isaac Haara, who had come to Vadsø from the Finnish settlement in Norbotten, Sweden. Anna and Isaac become parents to (Ida) Elmina, Jenny, Alma, Leander, and John. No information is known about Anna, born 1878, or Isaac, born 1883, so it may be assumed they did not survive infancy. A son Edward was born in Michigan in March 1895.

On October 21, 1891, Anna Haara and four children emigrated from Vadsø via Trondheim on the ship Domino, bound for New York and Michigan's Keweenaw Peninsula, which is the northernmost part of Michigan's Upper Peninsula. She rejoined her husband Isaac and daughter Elmina, who had emigrated in 1890 to marry Jacob Hepola. For a time the families lived together in company housing, then Isaac and Anna built a house at 145 Millionaire Street, Osceola (now considered to be in the town of Calumet, Michigan).

On September 7, 1895, the date of the Osceola mine fire, Anna became a widow at age 45. She buried Isaac in an unmarked grave in Lakeside Cemetery, Calumet, and soon moved to Menahga, Minnesota, with daughter Elmina's family. Later she moved to New York Mills where she raised her unmarried children.

Although the image of Anna resting is comforting, a postcard written in August of 1916 suggests that family and community demands were placed on her even later in life:

> Tell Grandma that Mrs. Kotaerkki wants her about
> the 1st of September. Of course Aunt Alma needs
> Grandma too. Martha is helping her at present.
> —In Haste, Esther Jonas

Anna Hepokoski Haara would earn her eternal rest at age 81, February 28, 1931.

Isaac Haara

The 1865 census of Vadsø, Norway, shows Isak Hara, born in 1845, a lodger at 120 Kvaenby Yttere, an unmarried 20-year-old Swedish Kven. He had been in Vadsø two years. Kvens were Finnish-speaking people who had traveled north to Ruija, "The Land by the Arctic Ocean," at a time of great famine and worked as farmers, miners, and fishermen. Settling first in Troms and Western Finnmark, from the 1830s they went mostly to the fisheries at Vadsø on the Varanger Fjord.

The 1875 census shows Isak Isaksen Hara, a fisherman and day laborer, among the 41 persons at 50, 39 Byens meliemste Deel. In this census he is not listed as a Kven. His birthplace shows Carl Gustavs Sogn Sverige (Sweden). He is married since 1869 to Anna Jacobsdatter Hepokoski, age 25, a Finnish Kven. They are parents of Ida Isaksdatter Hara, age five, and an infant, Jenny Isaksdatter Hara.

These emigrants to Vadsø kept their Finnish ways, bathing in the community smoke sauna and baking bread in the community brick oven. As payment, they left fresh loaves of bread and firewood, scarce in the barren Arctic landscape.

Perhaps a Michigan mining company agent who hired displaced Finns for jobs in the copper mines recruited Isaac for a job in the Osceola mine; his emigration date is unknown. Their oldest child, (Ida) Elmina, had emigrated to Michigan in 1890 to marry Jacob Hepola. Isaac sent for Anna and the other children in 1891.

The two families lived together in company housing until Isaac and Anna built a home at 145 Millionaire Street in Osceola on land leased from the mining company. An American-born son, Edward, arrived in March 1895.

Tragedy struck six months later. On September 7, 1895, Isaac was one of 30 men and boys lost in the Osceola mine fire, the worst mining disaster in Michigan history. He is buried at Lake View Cemetery at Calumet.

(Ida) Elmina Haara Hepola

The first of seven Norwegian-born children, (Ida) Elmina was born to Isaac and Anna Haara on December 6, 1870, in Keesberg, Norway, near Vadsø on the Varanger Fjord.

Family stories say that Elmina met Jacob Hepola when he worked as a farmhand in Vadsø. On October 18, 1890, Elmina emigrated from Vadsø via Trondheim, Norway, on the ship *Domino*, bound for New York and Osceola, Michigan.

She and Jacob Hepola were married in Osceola on January 10, 1891. Their children, born in both Minnesota and Michigan, were Mangna, Axel, Esther, John, Susan, Henry, Alma, Hilda, Jennie, Mary, Lempi, and Frederick.

In 1899, Jacob and Elmina Hepola moved from Michigan to Runeberg Township, Becker County, Minnesota. They traveled by train, bringing a wood-burning cook stove they bought at Keckonen Hardware Store in Calumet. Later, daughter Mangna moved this stove to the house she built across the field from the home place. It was also used by son Henry in logging camps in northern Minnesota. Mangna gave the stove to niece Virginia and Dick Fiegel for their home in Traverse City, Michigan. The stove has since traveled back to Minnesota and is at Kayo and Mel Kirchhoff's cabin at Hackensack until claimed by Mangna's namesake, Nell Mangna Kirchhoff.

In 1903, Jacob and Elmina and family moved to Wadena County, where the family homestead still stands. Elmina died on May 3, 1921, at Menahga, Minnesota.

Jacob Jacobson Hepola

In 1867, the year of Finland's worst famine, Jacob Hepola and Lisa Henrikintytar Hepola and their five children left Pudasjarvi, Finland, to ski 400 miles to Norway. Records from their church show that the family left "without documentation," that is, they were among many starving people who did not wait for permission from the church and fled in winter over frozen rivers, to find employment and food in the mines or fisheries of northern Norway. The routes were lined with bodies of people who died along the way. Jacob, age seven, born July 25, 1860, was the middle child.

They had lived and worked for a large farm outside of Pudasjarvi called the Hepola Farm and in Finnish tradition Jacob and Lisa had taken the name of the farm. Again following tradition, Jacob used the name Jacobsen in Norway and Jacobson for a short time in the United States.

To his children Jacob referred to himself as an orphan so we assume his parents died someplace in Norway. We have no record of where Jacob was from the time he was seven until he emigrated. Census records for Vadsø do not show a Jacob Hepola, but that means only that he was not there in 1865 or 1875, or that he was going by the name Jacobsen, a name we did not check in the census. Family stories indicate he met Elmina Haara when he worked as a farmhand in Vadsø.

Many young men left for America for economic, political or personal reasons. Jacob was among them, emigrating from Vardø via Trondheim on July 18, 1882, aboard the ship Hero and arriving August 4 at the Port of New York.

The route took him through a storm-tossed region where many ships were lost. A family story relates that he had arranged his departure but changed his plans, having received a warning in a dream that the ship would sink. He begged a neighbor who was scheduled to leave on the same ship not to go. She laughed at him; the ship sank and the woman was lost.

After a time this woman came to Jacob in a dream and said, "People complain that their bed in life is hard, but I am now sleeping on a bed of stone." Her body was found washed up on a rock along the rugged seacoast.

Looking at the dates of Jacob's emigration from Norway, we see he was 22 years old in 1882; Elmina would have been only 11. She joined him in Michigan in 1890 and they were married on January 10, 1891.

We are missing many details of his immigration journey. On March 5, 1890, before his marriage, he appeared before the Clerk of the District Court of the Fifteenth Judicial District for the State of Minnesota. He announced his intention to become a citizen of the United States and "to renounce forever all allegiance and fidelity to any Foreign Prince, Potentate, State or Sovereignty whatever, and particularly to Alexander III, Emperor of Russia whereof he is a subject."

We do not know how long he was in Minnesota. He showed a great affinity for farming. Since he experienced the famine in his childhood, perhaps his goal was to own land, raise his own meat and vegetables and never have to be hungry again.

Jacob and Elmina were married on January 10, 1891, at Osceola, Michigan. The marriage license application asked for Jacob's mother's maiden name, and he answered, "Not Known," showing he knew virtually nothing of his childhood history.

A search of the mining archives of Michigan Tech University at Houghton yielded the name of Jacob Jacobson on a battered notecard in the *J* category of employees, showing he had started work on May 8, 1893, for Hecla Mining Company, as shown here:

Please Fill Out This Blank and Return It to This Office Before December 1st, 1893

1. What is your real name, in full?
   Jacob H Jacobson

2. What is the name on your pay book and number?
   Same number 1197

3. What is your lead number? *1197*

4. Where do you work and for whom?
   Hecla for Thomas Wills

5. Where do you live? *Osceola*
   House No? *No Number*

6. How old are you? *33*

7. Are you married or single? *Married*

8. If married, how many children have you? *3*

9. How old is each of your sons?
   Twenty-two months

10. What relatives have you working for this company? *None*

11. When did you begin to work for this company?
    8th of May 1893

12. If you did not write these answers, who wrote them for you? *[space is blank]*

In 1899, the family moved to Minnesota with Anna, Elmina's widowed mother.

Johan Erikinpoika Nisula and Serafina Vahvasenpaa Lovisa

Johan Erikinpoika Vahvanen Nisula, 42, and Lovisa (Sofia) Serafina Vahvasenpaa, 38, and their four children, Emilia, Juho Vihtori, Hilma Vilhelmiina, and Aleksanteri traveled for three days by horse-drawn wagon from Karstula to Vaasa to emigrate to America, leaving on August 13, 1880. In America they used the name Anttila.

A group, some of them relatives, now owns the farmstead they left behind and is dedicated to using it for educational purposes. Stones from the savu sauna, the rock fence that stretched around their farmyard, and stones from the family hearth can still be found. Here birch, spruce, staghorn sumac and highbush cranberries grow on the rocky shores of Lake Vahvasenjarvi. The family regularly traveled to the town of Karstula by rowboat, where the oldest house, dating to the 1700s, belonged to Lovisa's family. It is now owned by the city and used for feeding and sheltering the needy.

There is an age discrepancy in the Finnish records that was possibly explained to us by officials at the emigration center. At age 13, a child entering the U.S. could be sent back to their country alone if immigration officials detected even a minor sign of weakness or illness. It is speculated that Johan and Lovisa thought Emilia might reach her thirteenth birthday by the time of emigration so to protect her they had her and her younger brother listed as two years younger than they actually were in case Emelia contracted an illness or infection on the crowded ship.

The family settled first in Hancock, Michigan. Daughter Emilia (Emma) is believed to have worked as a maid in Dollar

Bay, Michigan, and later as a waitress at Henning, Minnesota, where she earned enough to buy a team of horses and a buggy. A midwife, she delivered more than 300 babies, spoke English well and served as translator for the doctor. With her team and buggy she transferred patients for medical care from Sebeka as far away as Brainerd.

A family story tells that Emma walked from Wadena to Sebeka to file the claim for the Anttila family homestead, wading in the river for part of the trip.

In May 1889, Emilia (Emma) married August Mattila. She was age 22, he was 36. They had seven children, one of whom, Albert, died at an early age. John William (Willie), was the eldest (married Esther Hepola), followed by Melia (married Charlie Salmela); Emil (married Alma Gatzke); Hjalmer; Evelyn (married Edwin Kela), and Nellie (married Alfred Lundberg).

In the autumn of 1889, Sofia Anttila (nee Lovisa Serafina Wahvasenpaa) arrived in New York Mills, Minnesota, from Calumet, Michigan, with two children, Hilma Vilhelmiina (Minnie) and two-year-old Adla, staying during the winter with friends and relatives.

John Anttila (Johan Vahanen) arrived from Calumet, Michigan, in 1890 and rebuilt an old log cabin for their home on the Red Eye River near Sebeka. John Nissula Vahvanen Anttila died January 26, 1899.

Sophie (Sophia) Anttila died on October 7, 1927.

August Mattila died on November 20, 1944.

Emma Anttila Mattila died on December 27, 1959.

September 7, 1895

On September 7, 1895, Isaac Haara said goodbye to Anna, his wife of 26 years, and walked the short distance from his home on Millionaire Street to the Osceola copper mine. He began another arduous day as a trammer, a human donkey, an immigrant Finnish laborer who pushed loads of copper-bearing rock along iron rails to where it was hoisted to the surface.

By evening, his married daughter Elmina and five younger children would be fatherless. Edward, his 6-month old American-born son, would not remember his father. A few hours into the shift Isaac became a statistic, one of 30 fatalities of the worst disaster in Michigan mining history.

Now other great-grandchildren and I wonder about the details of that terrible day. Our story is filled with regret, wishing we had asked about family stories earlier, asked questions when our parents were alive.

More than a century later, the search is difficult. We work with sources left to us: mining records archived at Michigan Technological University in Houghton, Michigan, letters in old-style Finnish, marriage records, homestead and immigration records, books and newspapers. From scattered facts we must draw our own conclusions.

The death of Isaac Haara took place on the Keweenaw Peninsula of the U.P., the Upper Peninsula of Michigan. Here pine, birch, spruce, and maple forests stand in sharp contrast to scarred, littered landscapes, reminders of an economy once based upon copper mining. Tall smokestacks no longer emit smoke, shells of concrete buildings no longer serve a purpose. This breathtaking landscape and the remnants of the industry that suffocated Isaac Haara are part of the legacy the Keweenaw offers to my generation of descendants.

My mother often said, "My grandfather died in a mine fire. The officials sealed the mine." On that fateful day she was only

16 months old, too young to remember it. She grew up with the same family lore that I inherited.

As we grew older, great-grandchildren made multiple trips to search for the mine and to seek information about the fire. We spoke to people on the street, asked questions in stores and heard that same terse indictment: "They sealed the mine."

Did the mining company have so little regard for human lives that it acted to save its mine at the cost of unfortunate employees' lives? Until we discovered a book published in 1991 by Larry Lankton, Professor of History at Michigan Technological University, *Cradle to Grave; Life, work and death at the Lake Superior Copper Mines* (Oxford University Press), we had no solid information.

Lankton's account does not support the charge that the mine was sealed:

> Mine superintendent W. E. Parnall arrived at the No. 3 shaft an hour after the fire had been detected. . . . He had only one way of checking the fire's destruction: capping and sealing the shafts. But many men and boys were still underground . . . capping the shafts would end any chance of escape . . . Parnall opted not to cap any of the shafts for several hours, even though he personally believed, after only a short time, that all workers still underground had to be dead . . . he held off on sealing the No. 3 shaft until five o'clock. He left the others open and did not even seal them off the next day.

A coroner's jury was convened and heard testimony for three days, after which it issued its verdict:

> That the deceased came to their deaths by suffocation caused by smoke and gas from a wood fire. . . . We

believe that this fearful loss of life is due to the fact
that deceased did not realize the seriousness of their
danger, although from the evidence given this jury, we
find that deceased were duly notified. We exonerate
the mine officials from all negligence in this sad affair.

The controversy began immediately. The next issue of *The Daily Mining Gazette* in Houghton reported:

By some means it has spread abroad that the
management closed the No. 3 shaft too soon. In reply
to this, Capt. Parnell stated that he went to No. 5
shaft and waited until all the men as well as the
searching parties had come up, the latter of whom
reported that no man could then live underground;
that at 3 o'clock a man went down the ladder in No. 4
shaft as far as the 2nd level, but had to return and
reported no person could possibly be alive down
there. . . . The rumor may have arisen from the fact
that preparations were made to close down the shaft
soon after the fire was discovered, but it was not, as
before stated, then covered, that act being postponed
until after 4 o'clock. None of those present, among
whom were several who had friends and relatives in
the mine, appeared to doubt Capt. Parnall's
statement, or the wisdom of closing down the shaft
when it was closed.

A newspaper clipping from the files of the Houghton County Historical Society from September 7, 1957, carries this version of the events:

Sixty-two years ago, on Sept. 7, 1895, the Osceola
Mine Fire was discovered. It was about 9 a.m. when

the blaze was found on the 27 level of No. 3 shaft, an updraft digging. Only a few hours had elapsed before it burned its way quite a distance toward the surface, says Con Sullivan of Laurium, who retold the story of the fire this week.

> "At about 11 a.m., Superintendent William Parnall of the Bigelow mines ordered the shaft sealed at the surface. When this took place, the draft changed to a downward direction."

The Houghton County Historical Society at Lake Lindon, Michigan, has a sketch by an unidentified artist of the Osceola No. 6 shaft house, with these comments:

> In 1895 a fire broke out underground. In order to save the huge wooden timbers holding up the mine roof in the adits the company closed the shaft openings. This smothered the flames but also snuffed out 30 miner's lives. Bitterness against the company lasted many years amongst those who lost grandfathers, fathers, brothers and cousins in the fire.

A makeshift tribute marks the mine site: a picture of a crowd gathered on the day of the fire, a list of fatalities, and a sign: "The worst mine fire in the Copper Country's history occurred at this site on September 7, 1895 — The Osceola No. 3 Mine Fire. Thirty men and boys lost their lives."

Slowly the scarred surface is being smoothed over. Wildflowers bloom beside twisted metal reinforcing rods. Saplings grow through broken concrete foundations. Orange plastic fencing surrounds cave-ins. A rusted tramcar rests, half in and half out of the soil. I touch its cold surface and grieve for my great-grandfather and the family he left behind.

September 7, 2007

The fall landscape unfolded bit by bit as we drove north into the heart of Michigan's Copper Country. Tall, dark spruce towered over oak and maple trees already afire in crimson hues. Yellow birch simmered next to feathery tamaracks just beginning to lose their color. All around, this grandeur.

But we harbored a darker image inside; the nightmarish blackness of a mine-turned-tomb. In the worst disaster in Michigan mining history, the very timbers that shored up the Osceola copper mine to keep workers safe caught fire and emitted the smoldering smoke that suffocated 30 men and boys, Isaac Haara among them.

Family members had visited the Keweenaw Peninsula repeatedly over the years, drawn as on mystical missions, pilgrimages to the area where our immigrant ancestors first settled. On this early September day in 2007, five cousins and two spouses traveled together, determined to locate the grave of our great-grandfather, the sole relative left behind when the remaining family moved to Minnesota. At the Calumet Convention and Visitors Bureau we shared the best information we had: one note saying Isaac was buried "in the Company cemetery," another that he was in the "cemetery behind Sacred Heart Church, unmarked and unkept."

Our contact disregarded the company cemetery concept and dismissed the Sacred Heart lead as a "waste of time"; burial there was restricted to those of the Catholic faith. She gave us a brochure describing a cemetery organized in July 1894, one year before Isaac's death. The time frame seemed plausible, and we were encouraged by reading that this was "one of the best maintained cemeteries in the Upper Peninsula."

Driving the two miles west of Calumet on M-203, we had no problem locating Lake View Cemetery, covering 82 acres on the Michigan shore of Lake Superior. We were vaguely aware of a travel trailer parked across from the entrance and a man sitting at a folding table in the shade of a tree, but his presence had no significance to us at the time.

The gates of the iron fence were open, the office clearly marked. Elaborately carved monuments and modest gravestones rose from the gently rolling, wooded hillside where more than 32,000 persons are buried. Surely a spot tended so carefully would also have well-maintained records.

Greeting the small, resolute group that entered his office, Superintendent Dan Byykkonen cautioned that our efforts might be futile. Reliance on an outdated system for recording grave plots prior to 1900 could make it difficult or impossible to identify those sites today. Mr. Byykkonen offered to search in his computer; no Isaac Haara was listed there.

Next, he brought a timeworn black book from the back room, the master list of early burials in the order they occurred. Our spirits soared, and then fell. The page we sought was missing. Puzzled, but searching for options, Mr. Byykkonen offered, "There is one more place I can look."

He retrieved a very old and rather fragile volume from the vault. Sitting at his desk with two of our party hovering over his shoulder, he began scanning names. All at once my sister, Kayo, announced, "There he is! Isaac Haara, Section 12, Plot 2."

We were directed to Section 12, an area 120 by 160 feet in size. Mr. Byykkonen prepared a list and told us that if we found these names on marked graves we would know we were close to Plot 2: Anna Dalke, Harralas, Mrs. Henriksen, Peter Malmstrom, Henderson, Locke, John McDonald, Shelkin. We moved from marker to marker, scratching moss from inscriptions on aged monuments. No listed name appeared.

We reasoned that Plot 2 must be near the outer edge of Section 12 with other unmarked graves close by. Choosing a plausible spot for a photograph, we five great-grandchildren clustered together. My husband Harlan, seeking to compose a photo with identifying landmarks in the background, moved us forward and to the left, a site near two matching obelisks.

At that moment a pickup drove up and parked on the service road. A smiling Mr. Byykkonen emerged. Intrigued by the situation, he had continued searching and thus verified plot locations in 1895. Strolling over to us he said, "I see you found it." In response to our puzzled expressions, he continued, "You are kneeling at your great-grandfather's grave."

With that sobering revelation, everything changed. The nameless patch of earth became hallowed ground, a significant part of our heritage. We lingered, reluctant to leave, our happiness tempered by sorrow for the family that left this grave behind when they moved to Minnesota four years after the burial.

We wondered if it was possible to have a gravestone installed, and turned again to Dan Byykkonen. We were fortunate: by coincidence it was the one day of the week that Charlie Ryan, the man across the road with the travel-trailer office, was there to handle requests such as ours.

Over a picnic lunch at a nearby park we agreed upon simple wording for a granite marker:

Isaac Haara, 1844–1895, Died Osceola Mine Fire

With a start we realized that it was September 7, 2007, exactly 112 years to the day of our great-grandfather's death.

ENDNOTES

Mattila Family Timeline

The following timeline is based on information provided by Finnish genealogist Veikko Väätäinen (see page 71):

1668. Birth of Antti Sarvi-Sarve. His Sami family left the nomadic reindeer-herding life and began to farm in the Kuusamo, Finland, area. He died March 3, 1744. He married Valpuri, born 1670, died May 8, 1761. Their children were Pekka, born 1691; Anna, born 1694 (married Olli Aikio); Antti Sarve (Takkila), 1699–January 6, 1770; Elin 1709–March 30, 1785 (married Joha Ervasti, 1722–June 11, 1782).

Antti Sarvi-Takkila married Liisa, born 1702, died January 8, 1768. Antti and Liisa had three children, Pekka, born 1722; Antti, born 1724; Valpuri, born 1726 (married Heikki Filipinpka).

Antti Sarvi-Takkila (1699–January 6, 1770) married Anna Posio on January 16, 1757 (1724–March 7, 1757). Died two months after the birth of son Heikki on March 5, 1757.

Heikki Sarvi-Takkila-Sotaniemi (March 5, 1757–January 1, 1770) married Anna Sakkinen (March 16, 1757–March 24, 1826) on February 29, 1784.

May 25, 1822: Brita Kaisa Raistakka (mother of August Mattila) born, Kuusamo area, died March 15, 1897. (She would marry Matti Sotaniemi Mattila, born January 1, 1824.)

January 1, 1824: Matti Sotaniemi Mattila (father of August Mattila) born. He would marry Brita Kaisa

Raistakka. They were parents of August (January 6, 1853), Fredrik Aron (December 12, 1855); Heikki (Henry, June 18, 1860–December 3, 1930); Paavo Herman (December 1, 1862–March 30, 1936); and daughter Riika, birth date unknown, death estimated 1911.

January 6, 1853: Matti Aukusti (August) Mattila born to Matti Sotaniemi Mattila and Brita Raistakka Mattila, Kuusamo area.

December 12, 1855: Fredrik Aron Mattila born to Matti Sotaniemi Mattila and Brita Kaisa Raistakka Mattila, Kuusamo area.

1881: August Mattila left Kuusamo for America with his brother Fredrik Aron (Fred) Mattila.

1883: August Mattila and Fred Mattila moved to the Sebeka, Minnesota, area, where they homesteaded a farm and lived together for several years.

May 1889: Emma (Emilia) married August Mattila. They had seven children.

March 15, 1897: Brita Kaisa Raistakka Mattila died in Finland.

1900: Matti Sotaniemi Mattila, father of August, came to the Sebeka area at age 76, accompanied by sons Heikki (Henry, June 18, 1860–December 3, 1930), Paavo Herman (Herman, December 1, 1862–March 30, 1936) and daughter Riika, birth date unknown, death estimated 1911.

December 7, 1905: Matti Mattila died.

December 31, 1920: Willie Mattila and Esther Hepola
married at her parents' home, Menahga.

November 20, 1944: August Mattila died.

December 23, 1959: Willie Mattila died.

December 27, 1959: Emma Anttila Mattila died.

December 1, 1969: Esther Mattila died.

Acknowledgments

"After the Funeral" appeared in *The Talking Stick Volume 21: Nightfall*, Jackpine Writers' Bloc, Inc., Menahga, Minnesota, 2012.

"Bath Night at the Petersons" appeared in *The Talking Stick Volume 27: New Arrangements*, Jackpine Writers' Bloc, Inc., Menahga, Minnesota, 2018.

"The Bells of Karstula" appeared in *Kippis! A Literary Journal*, published by the Finnish North American Literature Association, Volume 6, No. 1, Summer 2013.

"Blood Lab Waiting Room, Mayo Clinic, Rochester" appeared in *The Talking Stick Volume 30: Reclaiming Life*, Jackpine Writers' Bloc, Inc., Menahga, Minnesota, 2021.

"Blueberry Woods Symphony" appeared in *The Talking Stick Volume 21: Nightfall*, Jackpine Writers' Bloc, Inc., Menahga, Minnesota, 2012.

"Coffee Can Treasure" appeared in *The Talking Stick Volume 31: Escapes*, Jackpine Writers' Bloc, Inc., Menahga, Minnesota, 2022.

"The Cut Glass Bowl" appeared in *The Talking Stick Volume 29: Insights*, Jackpine Writers' Bloc, Inc., Menahga, Minnesota, 2020.

"Did I Teach Too Long?" appeared in *The Talking Stick Volume 17: Vanishing Point*, Jackpine Writers' Bloc, Inc., Menahga, Minnesota, 2008.

"Downsized" appeared in *The Talking Stick Volume 20: Black & White*, Jackpine Writers' Bloc, Inc., Menahga, Minnesota, 2011.

"Fall's Fleeting Splendor" appeared in *The Talking Stick Volume 19: Forgotten Roads*, Jackpine Writers' Bloc, Inc., Menahga, Minnesota, 2010.

"Farm Home Supper" appeared in *The Talking Stick Volume 29: Insights*, Jackpine Writers' Bloc, Inc., Menahga, Minnesota, 2020.

"For I was Hungry . . ." appeared in *The Talking Stick Volume 25: Voices Past & Present*, Jackpine Writers' Bloc, Inc., Menahga, Minnesota, 2016.

"Heikki: 1860–1930" appeared in *The Talking Stick Volume 22: In Retrospect*, Jackpine Writers' Bloc, Inc., Menahga, Minnesota, 2013.

"The Memory Tin" appeared in *The Talking Stick Volume 24: Undercurrents*, Jackpine Writers' Bloc, Inc., Menahga, Minnesota, 2015.

"Night Vigil" appeared in *The Talking Stick Volume 25: Voices Past & Present*, Jackpine Writers' Bloc, Inc., Menahga, Minnesota, 2016.

"Onion Tears" first appeared in *The Talking Stick Volume 16: Finding the Words*, Jackpine Writers' Bloc, Inc., Menahga, Minnesota, 2007.

"Point of View" appeared in *Talking Stick Volume 18: Common Threads*, Jackpine Writers' Bloc, Inc., Menahga, Minnesota, 2009.

"Raised in a Chicken Coop" appeared in *School Days and Farm Chores: Tales from the Good Old Days in Northwestern Minnesota*, Hometown Memories, LLC, Hickory, North Carolina, 2016.

"The Sauna at Twelve-Foot" appeared in *Otter Tail Review Volume 3*, iUniverse, Bloomington, Indiana, 2009.

"Seasons of My Childhood" appeared in *Talking Stick Volume 26: Fine Lines*, Jackpine Writers' Bloc, Inc., Menahga, Minnesota, 2017.

"Spurned Heirloom" appeared in *Talking Stick Volume 26: Fine Lines*, Jackpine Writers' Bloc, Inc., Menahga, Minnesota, 2017.

"They Also Serve" appeared in *The Talking Stick Volume 22: In Retrospect*, Jackpine Writers' Bloc, Inc., Menahga, Minnesota, 2013.

"The Train to Hearst" appeared in *The Talking Stick Volume 22: In Retrospect*, Jackpine Writers' Bloc, Inc., Menahga, Minnesota, 2013.

"The Visit" appeared in *Talking Stick Volume 23: Symmetry*, Jackpine Writers' Bloc, Inc., Menahga, Minnesota, 2014.

"Waiting" appeared in *Talking Stick Volume 28: Broad Strokes*, Jackpine Writers' Bloc, Inc., Menahga, Minnesota, 2019.